The Sound of Whisper

When Yehuda Amichai Wrote Hebrew Poetry, and Later

A selection of other books by Yair Mazor:

Hounding the Hound of the Baskervilles
A Poetic Portrait of the Detective Novel

Poetic Acrobat:
The Poetry of Ronny Someck

Nocturnal Lament:
The Poetry of David Fogel and Modern Hebrew Poetry

Broken Twig:
The Poetry of Dalia Ravikovich and Modern Hebrew Poetry

Bridled Bird:
The Poetry of Nathan Zach and Modern Hebrew Poetry

The Flower and the Fury:
The Poetry of Yonah Wollach and Modern Hebrew Poetry

Who Wrought the Bible? Unveiling the Bible's Aesthetic Secrets

Israeli Poetry of the Holocaust

Somber Lust: The Art of Amos Oz"

Pain, Pining, and Pine Trees: Contemporary Hebrew Poetry

The Triple Cord: Agnon, Hamsun, Strindberg:
Where Hebrew and Scandinavian Meet

The Poetry of Asher Reich: Portrait of a Hebrew Poet

The Hidden Bible: Unearthing the Bible's Artistic Secrets

The Sound of Whisper:

When Yehuda Amichai Wrote Hebrew Poetry, and Later

YAIR MAZOR

HenschelHAUS Publishing, Inc.
Milwaukee, Wisconsin

Published by
HenschelHAUS Publishing, Inc.
www.henschelHAUSbooks.com

ISBN: 978159598-885-0
E-ISBN:978159598-886-7
LCCN: 2021953414

For Aman, Dr. Aman Attieh,
The dearest and most loyal among friends.

Wherever you go, I will go;
Wherever you lodge, I will lodge;
Your people shall be my people,
And your God, my God.

—Book of Ruth, 1, 16-18

Contents

PREFACE

Yehuda Amichai is the most celebrated aesthetic ambassador of contemporary Hebrew-Israeli poetry. Born in Germany in 1924 (—2000), he immigrated to Israel in 1935, where he wrote numerous volumes of poetry and stories, novels, and plays.

Among Amichai's volumes of poetry are the following: **Achshav Uvayamim Ha'akherim** (Now and In the Days to Come) the epic poem **Bagina Hatziburit** (In the Park; 1959), **Shirim** 1948-1962 (Poems 1948-1962; 1967), **Achshav Bera'ash** (Now, With Much Noise; 1971), **Hazeman** (Time; 1977), **Meakhorey Kol Zeh Mistater Osher Gadol** (Behind All of This A Great Happiness Hides; 1974), **Veloh Almenat Lizekor** (And Not to Remember; 1971), **Shalvah Gedola: She'lot Uteshuvot** (Great Tranquility: Answers and Questions; 1980), **She'at Hakhessed** (Time of Grace [Compassion]; 1982), **Me'adam Atta Ve'el Adam Tashuv** (You come from Man and You'll Return to Man, 1983); **Gam Kaf-Hayad Hapetukha Haiyta Pa'am Egrof** (Also the Open Hand Palm Was Once a Fist; 1990).

Amichai also published two novels: **Mi Yitneni Malon** (Who Will Give Me a Place of Rest?; 1971) and **Loh Me'akhshav, Loh Mikan** (Not From Now, Not From Here; 1975). His short story collections include **Baru'akh Hanora'ah Hazot** (In That Terrible Wind; 1961, and an enlarged edition in 1973) and **Pa'amomim Verakavot** (Bells and Trains; 1968), a volume of dramas that includes four plays.

Despite the fact that Amichai writes in other literary genres, his proclivities as a poet always emerge in his prose-fiction and drama. Whether Amichai wears the garment of a novelist, a storyteller, or a playwright, these garments are nothing but ephemeral disguises. He never entirely sheds the aesthetic attire of the poet.

The aesthetic rise of Amichai gathered momentum in the early 1950s during the **Dor Hapalmach** generation. **Palmach** is an acronym of the Hebrew words **pelugot machatz**, meaning the attack/commando troops [smiting troopers] of the Israeli military forces prior to statehood that led Israel's War of Independence (1947-1949). The writers who were aesthetically and historically associated with **Dor Hapalmach** wrote, as one of their leading poets, Hayyim Gouri put it, in first-person-plural (*goof-rishon-rabbim*). **Dor Hapalmach** writers poetically expressed the Israeli national experience during those hard yet inspiring days of fighting for the young state's independence. Thus, those storytellers, novelists and poets preferred the collective national experience over the personal, individual intimate experience.

Despite his proximity to the literary creators of **Dor Hapalmach** literature, Amichai never shared their first-person-plural poetics. Amichai's natural territory is the personal, intimate internal world of the individual, the poem's lyrical speaker. He was influenced by the aesthetics of poets such as W.H. Auden, T.S. Eliot, Rainer Maria Rilke, Gottfried Benn, Else Lasker-Schuller, David Fogel and, in general, the school of Imagism. While aesthetic influences obviously fertilized his writing, they never overshadowed his originality.

Preface

In a newspaper interview with Israeli poet Ronny Someck, Amichai professed his artistic credo that "a poem should be as natural as a path in the desert," created in the most natural way. In other words, the path's route is easy to walk through, or it is close to water sources, or it successfully satisfies the walker's (either human or beast) safety needs. Amichai's analogy between a poem and a path in the desert alludes to a reciprocal bond between the natural and the simple. Many of Amichai's poems evoke the impression of a natural, casual simplicity. But on close examination, they are far more aesthetically complex.

In his poetry, Amichai dexterously, almost cunningly, cultivates two simultaneous aesthetic systems or layers: a surface (epidermic) layer and a latent (cryptic) layer. The surface layer displays a simple sketch of the situation, the lyrical speaker's attitude and feelings, the metaphorical fabric, and the message that addresses the reader. It also establishes the starting point for the latent layer, which upon examination reveals aesthetic intricacy, complexity, and sophistication that can be systematically deciphered. In Amichai's typical poem, the epidermic-surface layer often exhibits surprising metaphorical patterns, such as comparing God's attempt to fix His world with a mechanic lying under an automobile, trying to repair its broken engine. It may contain salient sensual scenes, fluent syntactical patterns, and an intimate, understated tone of rhetoric that suggests a personal, informal confession. It might touch on fictional characters, such as lovers, a child, a soldier, or someone who hopelessly seeks his lost childhood; sweet reminiscences of the forsaken past; or a celebration of eroticism. He offers an appealing range of subjects: war, love, frustrated love, aging, reminiscences of childhood, reconciliation with disappointing reality, coming to terms with the past, the sunny but harsh beauty of the Land of Israel, missed opportunities, doomed encounters, suffocating sexuality, and seductive eroticism.

Such aesthetic components comprise the surface of Amichai's poems and are accessible and inviting in their simplicity. This accounts for the sweeping success and popularity of his poetry both in Israel and other countries. He gives even the most localized topics universal meaning. These surface characteristics make Amichai's poetry accessible to readers who enjoy reading poetry but are not trained as literary critics. Nevertheless, this surface simplicity doesn't reduce the challenging and appealing poetic sophistication adroitly concealed beneath the poem's surface or in the poem's cryptic layer.

Unlike his peer, the influential Israeli poet, Nathan Zach, Amichai is not engaged in public, poetic activism. He doesn't edit literary journals and publish articles advocating a particular aesthetic credo. Nor does Amichai embrace Zach's idea of dealing with emotions in an unemotional way. Emotion is a dominant factor of Amichai's poetry. He does not conceal emotion but exposes it on the surface of the poem. It is this immediate directness that make his poems so appealing. However, Amichai's poetry is far from being sentimental. Buried beneath the surface are intellect and irony. The interplay between these different attitudes helps to convey the author's intention and the meaning of the poem.

We keep saying, Amichai does this and Amichai does that, Amichai intends, Amichai means. Does he really, deliberately, intend, mean, and plan? Does our reading of Amichai's poem agree with his intentions? Although this question is certainly intriguing, it is not of much relevance to our study of the poems. This question is more relevant to a historical or psychological viewpoint that aims to trace, detect, and analyze the process of writing in order to get at the intentions behind the words. The interest of the literary critic is of another nature. The work of the literary critic starts when the work of the poet ends. The literary critic does not deal with the intentions that conceived the poem. The literary critic deals with the poem.

As T.S. Eliot put it, "To divert interest from the poet to the poem is a laudable aim." The poet is the only writer of his poem, but he is certainly not the only critic of his poem, sometimes not the most qualified one.

The following briefly analyzed poems (as numerous other poems by Yehuda Amichai) plausibly display the aesthetic meridians and latitudes of his poetics:

- Earthly themes, avoidance of lofty, elevated, "lordly" themes;
- Very personal intimate tone, restrained, "muted" rhetoric;
- Rhetoric that prefers the sound of whisper, notable at the dead of the night, even the loud victorious, triumphal fanfare of a noisy trumpet;
- The rare "aesthetic dexterity" to convey moving emotionality while prudently curbing it, without letting it metamorphosize into undesirable sentimentality;

- The singular capacity to address God in the most intimate fashion while taking the gallant liberty to scold God;
- Adopting the standpoint of intimate rhetoric of "I" instead of collective rhetoric and standpoint of "we";
- Forming innovative, creative metaphors and similes such as portraying the stones of thills that surround Jerusalem like a pack of wolves lurking in a bush, conspiring to attack Jerusalem ("Mayor");
- Portraying the terrestrial globe as transparent so the grandchildren can watch their grandfathers calmly floating on the floor of the ocean of the land of Jerusalem ("Forgetfulnes in the Wallies");
- "My eyes wish to stream to each other like two neighboring lakes"; (From "Six Poems to Tamar");
- "The world is awaken tonight/ lying on its bed and its eyes are wide open" (From "Six Poems to Tamar");
- "Your eyes are still warm like beds/ In which Time slept" (From "Six Poems to Tamar");
- The memory of my father is wrapped in white paper/ like a sandwich prepared for a work day" ("My Father")
- Forming the most amazing amalgamations which unite elements which are totally divorced from each other in "earthly" reality, such as "I wrapped my shirts and my agony" ("I smell the scent of benzine");
- "I'll place, your soul, young woman, in the palm of my hand/As my dead father placed the ethrog

[citron] in soft wool" ("I smell the scent of Ben-zine");

- "I will get up early to bribe the coming day/ So it will treat us kindly" (From "Six Poems to Tamar");
- "The curly beard of Rabbi Yehuda Halevi [a highly renowned Jewish poet and scholar, in Spain, in the Middle Ages]/ was a continuation of his dreams" (Yehuda Halevi).
- Practicing subtle irony that can be piercing, yet without being brutally blatant. Such is for instance the comment about the opening line of the well known Jewish prayer in memory of the dead: "God filled with mercy," Yehuda Amichai's poem states the following: if God would not have been filled with mery, perhaps some mercy could have been left for the human beings on earth.
- The syntax of the poems flows fluently like in an intimate conversation, not being chained and harnessed to stern, rigid, metrical formulas.
- Introducing the wars which were forced upon the young state of Israel (notably the war for Independence (1947-1949) not from a heroic perspective but always from the individual's speaker's personal perspective, one which consists of "blood, sweat and tears."
- Language which consists of "earthy" verbal "sediments", basic and humble themes while being joined by phrase from well-known Jewish prayers utilizing Yehuda Amichai's own poetic words, his language is not like a cypress but rather like a stone rolling down tiredly on a moderate slope, heading its last nest.

Tender is the Touch of the Poem
Reading in a Cluster of Poems by Yehuda Amichai

God Pities the Kindergarten Children

God pities the kindergarten children
He pities the schoolchildren less
And He does not pity the adults at all.
He leaves them alone
And sometimes they are forced to crawl on all fours

In the blistering sand,
To get to the first-aid station
And they are bleeding.

Perhaps He will pity the true lovers,
Will bestow mercy and will shade
Like the tree that shades the homeless
Who sleeps on a bench on the boulevard.

Perhaps we also shall give them
The last coins of grace
Which mother left us
So their happiness will protect us
Now and in the days to come

From *Shirim, 1948-1962*

The poem's title and its identical first line encourage and prod the reader to believe that God is, indeed, *El Maleh Rachamim*, God full of mercy (the title and first line of a well-known Jewish prayer). The kindergarten children seem helpless and vulnerable; therefore, they truly deserve God's pity and mercy. As the poem's title and first line manifest God's mercy, it is more than natural that the reader adopts a very positive attitude toward God. Accordingly, the reader cultivates positive expectations. Following this vein, the poem's very beginning prompts the reader to assume that the rest of the poem will continue to depict God as the embodiment of divine pity and mercy; consequently, the reader's initial expectations will be confirmed, fortified, and reassured.

Adopting this course of understanding, the reader will be surprised that the following line seems to negate both his understanding and expectations: "He pities the schoolchildren less." The fact that God "pities the schoolchildren less," questions and undermines the reader's previous assumptions. Should not God pity the schoolchildren just as He pities the kindergarten children? Should not God's pity be equally bestowed upon everybody? However, at this early stage of the reading, one may still justify God: as the schoolchildren are more mature than the kindergarten children and, therefore, less vulnerable. God does not find it necessary to give the schoolchildren the same amount of pity He does the kindergarten children. In light of this, the reader's initial understanding and expectations are intact but somewhat shaken.

It is the third line of the poem that shakes the reader's faith as it states that God "does not pity the adults at all."

Thus, at this stage of the reading process, one cannot argue that adults don't need God's pity, and therefore, God should not be denounced for denying it to them. The following depiction of the adults, who are left alone in a war-like situation, while they are bleeding and crawling on all fours in the blistering sand, makes more than evident the fact that they desperately need God's pity, which is stolen from them. Through a well-monitored process, Amichai uses the dynamic nature of the literary text. The reader's early understanding is gradually denied, and his early expectations are frustrated.

The initial appreciation of God is replaced with piercing criticism and the blatant rebuke of *j'accuse.* As the adults' portrayal concentrates on their crawling on all fours, an intriguing analogy is established between the crawling adults and the kindergarten children. The adults who crawl on all fours resemble babies or toddlers. This analogy emphasizes the adults' chastising agony as well as God's failure. The adults' helplessness is met by an indifferent God. The well-known Jewish prayer previously mentioned addresses God as "God full of mercy." Not in this poem. The traditional "God full of mercy" turns into God void of mercy. The process of literary dynamics-in which an early appreciation of God turns into a sarcastic denunciation and all previous favorable expectations are surprisingly denied—is greatly effective. Surprise becomes a means for the pet to get this point across. He gradually exposes and emphasizes this criticism against God.

At this stage of the poem, the narrator's critical message is loud and clear: God's failure is indeed of a double nature. First, God performs as a miserly merchant since

He strictly measures His mercy and does not distribute it equally. Second, God's calculations are wrong and unjust: He bestows His pity on the kindergarten children, who are protected by the adults, but He bestows no pity on the agonizing adults, who are yearning for help and protected by no one.

Thus, through a gradual process of literary dynamics, the meaning of the poem's title, and opening declaration go through a dramatic metamorphosis. "God pities the kindergarten children" no longer indicated God's laudable mercy, but rather ironically rebukes God's enraging lack of mercy.

The following stanza in the poem continues and strengthens the criticism against God:

Perhaps He will pity the true lovers,
Will bestow mercy and will shade
Like the tree that shades the homeless
Who sleeps on a bench on the boulevard.

This stanza exhibits both the narrator's question and wish: if God does not find it possible or worthwhile to pity the chastised adults, perhaps He will find it possible to pity the true lovers? After all, the true lovers possess their sheltering and shielding love; therefore, their need for God's pity seems rather modest, one that can be easily fulfilled and satisfied. Can't God be, at least, as merciful as a tree that shades the homeless? The analogy between the true lovers and the homeless suggests that the true lovers do call for some mercy.

However, the beginning of the poem's concluding stanza shows that even a modest request for God's mercy is ignored, and indifferently denied.

Perhaps we also shall give them
The last coins of grace
Which mother left us...

As the narrator suggests that "we"—the people, the human beings—shall pity the true lovers, by giving them "The last coins of grace/ Which mother left us," it is more than evident that God is not even as merciful as a tree. While a tree shades the homeless, God is not willing to extricate Himself from His hard-hearted indifference, and He ignores even the most humble request for pity. Thus, as the disappointed narrator realizes that the traditional and expected "God full of mercy" is indeed God without mercy, he converts his verbal complaint against God into a practical action. Since God refuses to fulfill His duty and to deliver His mercy, the narrator replaces God by offering his own mercy for those who yearn for it. The narrator's noble offer is greatly appreciated by the reader, who realizes that the narrator is willing to sacrifice his/her dearest possession—the last coins of grace that his mother left him/her. Accordingly, the reader puts the narrator on the highest pedestal: the narrator's generosity and his/her noble initiative call for the highest degree of admiration.

In light of this, should not the reader be more than surprised, or even astounded by the poem's final verses?

So their happiness will protect us
Now and in the days to come.

These final verses shed a surprising, ironic light on the narrator's generous offer. The narrator's seemingly noble sacrifice is indeed a misleading camouflage, nothing but a selfish investment: he/she aspires to support the true lovers because it may be beneficial. Accordingly, the seemingly caring narrator is exposed as an impostor, as a shrewd merchant; his/her willingness to protect the true lovers calls for a price—the true lover's protective love. What was earlier considered a noble offer is later revealed as a cunning trade, a sly business of give and take. Consequently, the piercing, ironic accusation leveled at God by the narrator, boomerangs and hits the narrator himself/herself.

Once the reader realizes the narrator's cynical, sly pretending, the reader understands that the surprising metamorphosis was actually anticipated earlier, although subtlety. The true portrait of the narrator was hinted at by the fact that he/she is eager to support the true lovers, but not the agonized adults.

While he/she offers his/her last "coins of grace," he/she addresses this offer to the true lovers only, neglecting the suffering adults. Furthermore, the use of coins as a metaphor predicts the later portrayal of the narrator as a shrewd merchant. The fact that the poem's surprising punch line is subtly predicted in these two references does not undermine its surprising potency, but rather enriches it with a sophisticated touch.

The narrator's misleading mask is herby removed and his/her true nature is fully revealed: he not only shares God's indifference to human misfortune but also is selfish and hypocritical. The final exposure of the narrator is also the final exposure of the poem's textual dynamics. In its first stages, the poem cultivates a favorable attitude toward a God full of mercy. The second stage denies that early assumption. While God is found void of mercy, the narrator is found full of mercy. The third stage denies the assumption that the narrator is full of mercy by exposing him/her as not only as merciless as God, but also a shrewd impostor and a cunning hypocrite.

Amichai's prudent usage of the dynamic quality of the literary text is far from being just a literary device, a vain demonstration of literary dexterity. This dynamic connects the text to the poem's ideology, which is a bitter complaint against a bare world, empty of mercy, a world in which God and man yield nothing but indifference. The critical irony that results from the gulf between the early assumptions of the reader and their later denial, between the nursed expectations and their later frustration, stresses the poem's complaint and fortifies its bitterness. "When the poor have cried, Caesar has wept," says Anthony. When the poor cry, God and man are deaf, says Amichai, and his narrator is as honorable a man as Brutus. xxx

While the following poem does not display the intricacy of *Elohim Merakhem Al Yaldey Hagan* (God Pities the Kindergarten Children), the poet once again plausibly uses the dynamic of assumptions and their denial to fortify its deeper meaning.

Mayor

It is sad
To be the Mayor of Jerusalem
It is terrible.
How can any man be the mayor of a city like that?
What can he do with her?
He will build, and build, and build.

And at night
The stones of the hills round about
Will crawl down
Toward the stone houses,
Like wolves coming
To howl at the dogs
Who have become Man's slaves.

From *Shirim, 1948-1962*

The dynamics of the literary text in this poem also proves a useful tool to convey the poem's prevailing message. The poem opens with the following statement: "It is sad/ To be the Mayor of Jerusalem." This kind of declaration certainly calls for an explanation.

Why is it sad to be the mayor of Jerusalem? Should not one be excited, or even enthusiastic, to act as a mayor of such a unique city? Should not one feel privileged to be the mayor of a city that is undoubtedly the most sacred in the world? Being a mayor of Jerusalem seems a desirable zenith for a person of ambition and vision. Thus, the poem's first line erects not just bewilderment, but also a confusion that calls for an explanation. The next line, however, instead of explaining the previous confusing statement, adds to the confusion. How can it be "terrible" to be the mayor of the most exalted and inspiring city in the world? The initial expectations of the reader are herby blatantly frustrated. Armed with a mounting curiosity and goaded by a rising confusion, the reader eagerly reaches for the next line, which may clarify.

"How can any man be the mayor of a city like that?" Although this line does not directly provide a full answer to the previous question, it seems to channel the reader toward a possible answer. Jerusalem is not only a most sacred city, but it is also a city that one person cannot truly control. Jerusalem is like the eye of the storm, a center for countless conflicts and endless contradictions. Being the most sacred city for three leading religions, being in the very heart of the national and military conflict between Israelis and Arabs, Jews and Muslims, Jerusalem is not an easy city to control.

Jerusalem is an intersection of ideological conflicts, cultural contradictions, national struggles, political fights, religious rivalries, and conflicting interests. Jerusalem is a crossroads where all kinds of human conflicts meet and clash. Therefore, it is not only sad to be the mayor of Jerusalem, it is not only terrible to be the mayor of Jerusalem, it is probably impossible to be the mayor of Jerusalem. It is beyond human powers to tame a city like Jerusalem. This explanation seems to satisfy the reader's need for a rational answer to clear up the confusion. The bumpy literary dynamic seems also to reach a point of release and serenity.

However, this pacified sense of release and serenity does not last very long, it is quickly abandoned and disrupted by a new bewildering statement: "He will build, and build, and build." This verse seems at odds with reason. If Jerusalem, in its present size, is already untamable, it is already impossible to control, what is the point of building her bigger and bigger? The bigger Jerusalem, the bigger the problems. The poem's previous bewildering confusion, is herby replaced by a paradox. Thus, "turbulent" literary dynamics speak out again.

Naturally, the reader is eager to read the following verses, expecting that they will cast a reasoning light on the paradox and crack it:

And at night
The stones of the hills round about
Will crawl down
Toward the stone houses,
Like wolves coming
To howl at dogs
Who have become Man's slaves.

Paraphrasing these verses robs them of their spellbinding, nocturnal enchantment: the metaphorical depiction of the stony, somber mountains, lurking in ambush like wild wolves questing for prey, dramatically yields a tense, Gothic atmosphere, a sense of threat and suspicion. However, behind the verses' nocturnal beauty lies the logical sense of the paradox. The metaphor of the wild wolves, which threaten the domesticated dogs, emphasizes the second metaphor in this stanza, the one that deciphers the paradox and unearths its inner logical meaning. The second metaphor draws an imaginary situation in which the wild stones of the mountains surround Jerusalem, crawl down towards her, and threaten the domesticated, tamed stones of which the houses of Jerusalem are built.

This metaphor switches and shifts the poem's track by channeling it from a concrete layer towards a metaphorical layer. Thus, the paradox in focus may be reasoned and deciphered on a metaphorical level rather than on a concrete one. Accordingly, Jerusalem is constantly under an intimidating threat: the stony mountains around Jerusalem, display an unrestrained animosity toward the stony houses of Jerusalem, and threaten to invade and to destroy them. Therefore, the houses of Jerusalem are not only under an external threat, they are also feeble, meager, almost fragile, in comparison to the stony mountains around Jerusalem.

In light of this, the seeming paradox—"He will build, and build, and build"—makes perfect sense: as Jerusalem is so feeble, meager and frail, the only way to protect her, to shield her, to fortify her, is to build, and build, and build. The more one builds Jerusalem, the more he uses the wild stones of the mountains around Jerusalem. This way, by a constant building of Jerusalem, the wild, threatening stones become fewer and weaker, and correspondingly, their threat to destroy Jerusalem is weaker. The deciphered paradox plays a prominent role in the poem's literary dynamics. The late information sheds a dramatic new light on the way the early information was comprehended by the reader.

The reader's understanding of the poem prior to confronting the paradox was the following: Jerusalem is a worldly intersection in which countless conflicts meet, wrestle, and clash. Thus, the everlasting, acute problems of Jerusalem make this city untamable and almost impossible to control. Therefore, it is sad, it is terrible, and it is impossible to control Jerusalem. However, as the reader deciphers the later paradox, while reaching the poem's ending, he/she is surprised to find out that the present understanding of the poem is wrong indeed. It is not impossible to control Jerusalem because of the city's untamed, powerful nature, but rather because of the city's feeble, fragile nature. The countless conflicts in Jerusalem don't make the city wild, harsh, turbulent, and powerful – according to the poem's early interpretation – but rather torn, worn out, and ramshackle.

As in the previously discussed poem by Amichai, the misleading literary dynamics is far from being, just a flashy prank, a dexterous demonstration of verbal juggling void of meaning. Amichai's literary dynamics do not lead astray in vain: it deftly mobilizes the surprising gap between the early reading and the late reading, in order to make a point, in order to underline an idea, in order to deliver a message. The literary dynamics, then, is nothing but a rhetorical tool that is harnessed to the poem's prevailing ideology. By leading and guiding the reading process in the zigzagging manner of trial and error, Amichai sheds brighter light on the poem's meaning.

Like many Jerusalem poems by Amichai, "Mayor" is also a lover's lament. Jerusalem is really impossible. She is as frail as eternal. Jerusalem is the age-old capital of Israel, and she is the age-old capital of conflicts. Jerusalem is united by her conflicts and torn by them. The poem's paradox is cracked and deciphered. Through hundreds of generations, Jerusalem was destroyed, and destroyed, and destroyed and destroyed; through hundreds of generations, Jerusalem was built, and built, and built. Jerusalem collects conflict, sorrow and pain, like people who collect coins and stamps. But Jerusalem not only collects conflicts, sorrow, and pain, Jerusalem also collects love. The conflicts, the sorrow, the pain, which Jerusalem collects, make her frail, make her impossible. The love that Jerusalem collects, makes her possible, makes her eternal. This love is also expressed in Amichai's poem. The weakness of Jerusalem turns into the strength of this poem. The weakness of Jerusalem feeds the poem's emotions.

Amichai doesn't recoil from exposed emotions. Unlike Zach, who locks emotions in the most cryptic layer of the poem, Amichai lets emotions invade and populate the poem's surface. However, Amichai never leaves emotions bare and exposed, rather he anchors them to a literary mechanism that shapes and molds them to fit in the poem's thematic fabric, to meet with the poem's ideological credo. Emotions, in Amichai's poetry, are not only well-controlled, but are also deftly monitored, toward a smooth assimilation within the various aesthetic tissues of the poem. As much as emotions are exposed in Amichai's poetry, they never deviate from a well-measured dosage.

The two poems in focus seem to demonstrate how a collaboration between emotions and a well-monitored literary mechanism, such as literary dynamics, result in a correct poem indeed. Amichai's correct poem differs from Zach's correct poem, but it is no less correct. (The term "correct poem" was coined by Zach.)

Numerous poems by Amichai address the issue of war, a subject fraught with emotion. However, in his war poems, Amichai displays an impressive capacity to bridle emotion while keeping sentimentality in check. Sentimentality may be defined as an overwrought deteriorating state of emotionality. Amichai's war poems, however, skillfully maintain a line between aesthetically tolerable emotional expression and undesirable sentimentality. The following discussion aims to pay homage to Amichai's impressive aesthetic dexterity.

One may convincingly argue that all art is besieged by an intriguing paradox. A considerable part of any work of art is founded upon emotion. Even the most ambitiously intellectual, logical artistic creation that aspires only to analytical insight is not completely devoid of emotion. Such a lack would undoubtedly devitalize the piece, leading to shallowness. Thus, emotion is not only laudable but crucial to any work of art. When feeling deteriorates into over-emotionality, when the delicate balance between depicted object and artistic depiction is upset or destroyed, the work suffers. The artistic paradox is therefore enticing and potentially devastating at the same time: the creative work's vitality and its deterioration spring from the same source, and the dividing line between the two may be hazy. In most cases, though, readers seem to possess a reliable capacity to distinguish correctly between moderated emotion and exaggerated sentimentality.

Perhaps it is easier to demonstrate a methodology for avoiding sentimentality than it is to define the difference between subtle emotion and coarse sentimentality. Good art creates an equilibrium between the emotional resonance evoked by the subject and that of the artistic depiction. This goal may be achieved by a deftly calibrated process of restraining emotions and distilling sentiments.

One might contend that distancing is easier to establish in literature, the verbal art, than in the other arts. This argument is based on the fact that the distance between the artistically molded reality and the molding medium is greater in literature than in, say, painting, sculpture, music, or dance. Color, form, sound, and movement are all physical phenomena; words are the only artificially creative materials not found in nature. This unique character of the verbal arts is acknowledged by the Psalmist, who lauds: "The heavens declare the glory of God; and the firmament sheweth His handiwork. Day unto day uttereth speech, and night unto night sheweth knowledge. There is no speech nor language, where their voice is not heard" (Psalms 19, 1-4). The verbal personification that the psalmist bestows upon nature maintains the only thing it does not possess: words.

More than prose-fiction or drama, poetry seems to shrink literature's inherent distance between depicted object and depicting medium because poetry more strongly prefers emotional to rational expression. Prose-fiction, especially the novel, is the most conscious and intellectual literary form: it doubts, examines, muses, inquires, suspects, expounds, probes, and analyzes. Poetry is more likely to express emotion; therefore, the need to curb emotions and block sentimentality in poetry becomes an urgent one. This need increases when the poet's subject itself is highly charged, such as war. And when it comes to war in Hebrew poetry, the name Amichai rises.

Although war is not the most predominant component in his work, his poetry does embrace all Israeli wars from the War for Independence through the war in Lebanon. Furthermore, Amichai's poetry displays a flexible and sensitive capacity to modify literary means according to alternating emotional reverberations emerging from different wars. The unique feelings generated by the Six-Day War and the Lebanon War in comparison to the War for Independence are prudently mirrored in his verse, and his work may be considered a poetic, historical account as well as a sensitive moral barometer of Israel's conflicts.

As previously mentioned, Amichai's poetry differs markedly from Zach's yet ardently exemplifies Zach's axiom: "when sentiment fades away, the correct poem speaks out." Amichai uses a repetitive technique in his poetry, adopted to avoid sentimentality. Although a poem's focus may be war and its agonizing outcome, the subject is treated not directly but obliquely. Thus war is evasively depicted through themes and topics that are relatively divorced from war itself. Consequently, war is uprooted from its highly charged context. In other words, Amichai deflects attention from a given war, insulates its emotional potential, and thereby establishes aesthetic distance.

This technique is proficiently displayed in the following sonnet, which opens a group of sonnets titled *Ahavnu Kan* (We Loved Here):

My father spent four years in their war
And neither hated his enemies not loved them;
But I know that already there
He built me day by day from his tranquilities
Which have been so few, collected by him
Between bombs and smoke,
And he put them in his worn bag
With the rest of his mother's drying cake.

And he collected in his eyes nameless dead
Many dead he collected for me,
For I will recognize them in his looks and will know them

And I will not die like them in the atrocity-
He filled his eyes with them and he was wrong:
I continue going to all my wars.

From "Poems" 1948-1962

The poem's major theme is the narrator's own forced participation in war despite his father's hopes, but it is suspended by the poem's end and, consequently, is considerably blurred. One may also discern a rhetorical device we might call thematic swindling. The reader assumes that the father's wars are the poem's focus, only to realize at the poem's conclusion that he/she has been misled. This switch frustrates expectations, giving the poem an enigmatic tinge and making an intellectual deciphering necessary. The reader must extricate the poem from the emotional level to reach the rational one, and, therefore, the emotional potential is weakened.

Furthermore, the majority of the poem is devoted to the father's wars. Despite their horrors, they deflect attention from the narrator's wars and thus blunt their impact in the poem. A similar thematic defection is demonstrated in *Shir Al Hakravot Harishonim* (A Poem on the First Battles):

On the way to the front we stayed overnight
in a kindergarten
Under my head I put a woolen teddy bear
Upon my tired face dreidels descended
And trumpets and dolls-
Not angels,
My feet, in heavy boots
Let fall a tower of colorful dice
Which have been put each on the other,
Each die smaller than the one under it
And in my head big and small memories
confusingly mingled
And made dreams.
And beyond the window there were fires...
And also in my eyes under my eyelashes.

Here thematic deflection seems to reach a level of extreme elaboration. Though war is again the poet's center of interest, it is left to a relatively marginal part of the poem and alluded to only hastily. In *Ahavnu Kan* (We Loved Here), the narrator's war is suspended until the end, whereas in the present example the war is inlaid from the very beginning and then blatantly abandoned. The dilution of war's emotional potential is achieved through a diversion of attention from war to a kindergarten. The naïve and peaceful connotations thus evoked soften the harsh, devastating impact of armed conflict. On the other hand, the encounter emphasizes the horrors of war when contrasted to the tranquil background of the kindergarten. The shift mutes the emotional response generated by war but does not let emotionality completely dissipate. Consequently, the poem's emotional tone is balanced.

Another example of Amichai's skillful use of thematic deflection to control inordinate emotionality is found in *Bet Hakevarot Hatzva'i Habriti Behar Hatzofim* (The British Military Cemetery on Mount Scopus).

Forgetfulness in the valleys.
More remembrance on the mountain.
A diligent prudence constructed
On the mountain slopes. How can one die
At a great distance for
A country that does not exist? And I
Was not born then, yet.
Sometimes in summer
When the terrestrial globe is transparent,
The grandchildren of those who died watch
Their dead grandfathers calmly floating
As on the floor of the ocean
Of the land of Jerusalem.

From *And Not to Remember*

The British wars in Israel took place many decades ago, and their selection as the poem's theme already establishes a certain historical distance. Still, since British rule in Israel is historically bound to the Israeli struggle for independence, the emotions aroused by the war have not completely faded. Thus, the War for Independence saliently echoes between the poem's lines, but its emotional resonance is muted. Moreover, the narrator's reference to the British-killed soldiers as grandfathers serves as a cunning device of temporal displacement and cultivates the illusion that they continued to live after death, as young men, and eventually became grandfathers. The temporal remove and the illusion of survival function together to lessen the sorrow of the soldiers' death and consequently reduce its emotional impact.

The same technique is well demonstrated in one of a group of poems titled *Kinot Al Hametim Bamilkhama* (Lamentations on the War Dead):

The memorial of the unknown soldier is
On the other side. The enemy's side.
A good reference point for the artillery men
Of the future.

Or the war memorial in London
Hyde Park corner, decorated as a cake
Fancy and rich: one more soldier raises his head

And a gun, one more cannon, one more eagle, one more
Stone angel.
And a big marble flag like whipped cream
Poured from above
Artistically
The over-sweet cherries
Too red
Already have been gluttonized by the glutton of hearts.
Amen.

From *Behind All This A Great Happiness is Hidden*

Although the poem begins with reference to what was probably an Israeli unknown-soldier's memorial, erected in haste during the battles and now beyond the border on the enemy's side, the focus shifts rapidly to a British war memorial in the heart of London. That depiction of the British monument, so different from the Israeli one, occupies most of the poem's text and closes the piece. The coquettish richness of the foreign memorial confronts the meekness of the Israeli monument. Whereas the latter is bleakly besieged on the enemy's side, the former is proudly located in the center of the city, declaring its arrogant artistry. Furthermore, the foreign memorial is made of stone, symbolically announcing that the war and its horrors are also now petrified, never to return. In contrast, the Israeli marker is described as a good target for artillery men in future conflicts. The foreign war came to an end;

the Israeli one did not and is augured to continue as bloody as ever.

Imagining the Israeli memorial as a convenient target for future marksmen is also bitingly ironic: the soldiers who were shot and killed are doomed to repeated shellings after their death. Even the tomb cannot provide the repose they never found while alive. Another ironic barb is directed at the foreign monument. The British role in Israel during the years prior to the War for Independence was certainly not laudable, despite lofty pretensions of bringing order and relative stability to the region. Now British rulers have erected a grandiose memorial to commemorate their army's service, while the war they pretended to end goes on. Such irony is not only ideological, but also acts as a tool to curb sentimentality by establishing an emotional distance, leading to clear-eyed rationality.

Amichai also restrains sentimentality with verbal simplicity, a sort of rhetorical meekness, as in *Geshem Bisdeh Hakerav* (Rain on the Battlefield).

Rain falls on the faces of my friends;
On the faces of my living friends who
Cover their heads with a blanket
And on the faces of my dead friends who
Do not cover any more.

The simple, ordinary language and the modest tone of this short poem create a considerable distance between emotional essence and rhetorical utterance. A cry becomes a whisper; weeping all but vanishes. Potential sentimentality therefore fades, and a very "correct poem," following Zach's prescription, results. The dead and the living are equal because the rain soaks everyone. That horrible equality is again shown as the live soldiers cover their faces with blankets and look like their dead comrades-who are customarily covered with a blanket on the battlefield. The enormous emotional impact born of such statements demands drastic restraints.

Monitoring the language and tone seems an appropriate rhetorical technique for the poem's aesthetic needs. The analogy between the living and the dead soldiers (which stems from their unexpected changing roles: the living soldiers cover their heads with a blanket and correspondingly look dead while the dead soldiers are not covered and thus look alive) yields further aesthetic complexity as it is mirrored on the level of syntax. Accordingly, the same syntactical structure portrays both living and dead soldiers. That and more.

The poem amalgamates death and water (rain). Such an amalgamation evokes two Biblical allusions that also combine death and water: the flood, and the Egyptians drowning in the Red Sea. The fact that the poem prudently and deftly enlists and echoes two Biblical allusions not only contributes to its aesthetic dexterity but also endows the poem with a universal, historical touch. What happened in the distant, misty past continues occurring in the present. The fact that water is traditionally associated with life (while in the poem and in the Biblical allusion water heralds death) yields surprisingly paradoxical irony that further underscored the poem's lament about everlastingly conducted wars.

The same verbal monitoring applies to the metaphorical texture of another poem from *Kinot Al Hametim Bamilkhama* (Lamentations on the War Dead):

Dikki was hit
Like the water tower in Yad Mordechay
Hit. A hole in the belly. Everything
Streamed out of him.

But he remained standing like that
In the landscape of my memory,
Like the water tower in Yad Mordechay.

Not far from there, he fell
A bit northward, near Chulekat.

From.*Behind....*

Poetry's exalted, celebrated verbal characteristics are missing here, replaced by a surprising simplicity in which a dying soldier is compared to a collapsing water tower. The customary elevation of figurative language is not completely abandoned, however, for a dryly reported simile, which could have been taken from an informative newspaper account, attains its rhetorical purpose. The rhetorical impact resembles one of a bored tourist guide who monotonously-almost indifferently-points out place after place. The holy becomes secular, the divine becomes earthy, and the emotionally laden poem escapes sentimentality.

Elsewhere, simile gives way to metaphor, and the hierarchic relationship between the metaphorically related elements acts as a cornerstone for rhetorical restraint, as in the fourth poem of *Kinot Al Hametim Bamilkhama* (Lamentations on the War Dead):

I found an old book about animals,
Brehm, second volume, birds;
In a sweet language, depiction of a starling's life,
A thrush and a swallow. Many errors in an old

Gothic script, but a lot of love. "Our winged
Friends," "Wandering from us to the warm countries,"
A nest, a spotted egg, soft down, the nightingale,
The stork, "The spring harbingers."
The red chest.

Year of publication, 1913, Germany,
The eve of the war which was the eve of my wars:
My good friend who died in my arms and his blood
In the dunes of Ashdod, 1948, June.

Oh, my friend
The red chest.

From...*Behind...*

The metaphorical bond between the robin's red breast and the blood-covered chest of the speaker's friend is cleverly wrought and meaningfully baffling. The poem's first two stanzas lead the reader to assume the poem's focus is an old, alluring German bird book. The third stanza then connects the book's date of publication to World War I, provoking the reader's curiosity, and further links that war to the Israeli War for Independence. The German defeat in World War I produced the Germany that started World War II; the Jews who escaped that war and reached Israel were later forced to fight for independence. Only the poem's closing stanza fully reveals the true focus, however, and the reader's frustrated assumptions compel him/her to reread and reconsider the poem. The bird descriptions, especially the red breast, are not the thematic nucleus, as previously believed, but only a vehicle for the metaphor in which the narrator's dead friend (whose chest turned red from blood) is at the center.

This zigzag process of literary comprehension is certainly not unique. Many literary texts deliberately dictate a reading-comprehension process whereby later information casts new light upon previously rendered information and, consequently, alters the initial perception of meaning.

As Wolfgang Iser says, "The act of reaction is not a smooth or continuous process, but one which, in its essence, relies on interruptions of the flow to render it efficacious. We look forward, we look back, we decide, we change our decisions, we form expectations, we question, we muse, we accept, we reject; this is the dynamic process of reaction." However, in Amichai's poem, the reading process is prudently mobilized for the rhetorical goal of preventing sentimentality: its baffling characteristics condition a drastically rational reaction that eliminates its emotional potential. In other words, the reader's reaction to the poem is extricated from the emotional level and directed to the rational level, enabling sentiment without sentimentality.

Irony and sentimentality cannot coexist. Excess emotionality is based on a lapse of critical distance; irony springs from that distance. The attainment of such distance becomes more problematic as Amichai's thematic focus shifts from the struggles for independence (1947-49) and the Yom Kippur War (1973) to the recent conflict in Lebanon, the most confusing and most heatedly debated war Israel has ever known. This war is painfully different from, and far worse than, previous ones; it aspired to bring peace, yet is still continues yielding death and destruction. Some argue that although the conflict erupted in 1982, its roots can be traced to the Six-Day War (1967). The consequences of that war were dramatic and even spectacular. The haunting sense of a besieged country threatened constantly by animosity was drastically alleviated. The stifling, perpetual fear of destruction was suddenly replaced by glorious self-confidence. The constricted borders, exposed to constant attacks, were expanded through enormous conquests from horizon to horizon. Victory was not easily digestible, however. The sharp transition from a state of siege to sweeping conquest also overcame any sense of modesty. Pride, excessive self-confidence, and a vain haughtiness arose. David not only smote Goliath but also succeeded him.

The traumatic Yom Kippur War was the bitter result of those perilous developments. Still, the lesson was not learned. Grief and blatant rage surfaced during the summer of 1982. Indeed, hostile foes of yesterday turned into willing peace-seekers, whom Israel embraced. However, even the absence of Egypt and Jordan from the "battle belt" did not radically alter the vicious calculus of enmity in which Israel is still the threatened component. Israel's basic struggle for survival was no less right than before, but the protracted Lebanon conflict raised more questions than answers. Indeed, Israel's role in the chaos of Lebanon is far from calling for laurel wreaths; the blood of the innocent victims is still calling from the troubled ground of Lebanon. The painful nature of Israel's most recent war is piously mirrored in the following poem:

The Real Hero of the Hagedah/Ha'ag Isaac's Sacrifice

(*Hagibor Ha'amiti Shel Ha'aqedah*)

The real hero of the aqedah was the ram
Who did not know about the conspiracy among the others
As if he volunteered to die instead of Isaac.

I want to sing him a memorial poem,
About the curly wool and his human eyes
About the horns that were so quiet on his vibrant head
*And after he was slaughtered they made of them shofarot**
For the cheering of their war
Or for the cheering of their vulgar happiness.

I want to remember the last scene

* blowing horns

Like a handsome photograph in a refined fashion journal:
The tanned young man, indulged in coquettish clothes
And next to him the angel dressed in a long silk garment
For a celebrated reception.
And they both stare with empty eyes
At two empty seats
And behind them, like a colorful background, the ram
Held in the thicket before slaughter.
And the thicket is his last friend.

The angel left for home
Isaac left for home
And Abraham and God left long ago

But the real hero of the aqedah
Is the ram.

From... *Time of Grace*

Though the aqedah story has inspired numerous variations, both in Hebrew and non-Hebrew literature, Amichai's approach to this ancient yet fresh and tantalizing motif is striking: all the traditional participants in the sacrificial drama are bypassed, and the ram, the real victim, is elevated to a leading role. This surprisingly innovative interpretation is not superficial manipulation or vain literary provocation but a useful vehicle to render a critical message.

The specific nature of this message is clarified in the last three lines of the first stanza: “And after he was slaughtered they made of them *shofarot* / For the cheering of their war / Or for the cheering of their vulgar happiness.” These lines refer to the euphoria that flowed from the intoxicating victory of the Six-Day War. Associating the *shofarot* (ram’s horns, which are blown during the Jewish High Holidays) with that “vulgar happiness” expressly recalls the sounding of the ram horns after the conquest of the Wailing Wall during the Six-Day War, a celebration that the poet interprets as a disturbing sign of presumptuousness. The phrases ”*their* war” and “*their* vulgar happiness” manifest his recoil from such conceited behavior, in which he wishes no part.

A common denominator between Amicai’s critically scolding elucidation of the aqedah and his denunciation of the Six-Day War’s unfortunate consequences is clear, however: there are always forsaken victims who pay for others’ happiness with their lives. In this sense, the slaughtered ram and the young soldiers who fell during the war are analogous sacrifices sharing analogous altars. The word volunteered (*hitnadev*) is particularly significant, since volunteerism is a key concept in regard to the Israeli army. The term may thus be considered an integrative element that binds past and present, the fable to its moral. An identical expressive connection springs from the change in verb tense between the opening and closing lines of the poem: “The real hero of the *aqedah* was the ram...the real hero of the *aqedah* is the ram.” The biblical ram was sacrificed in the distant past; its young human successors are being continually sacrificed today. Past and present are bound in bloody redundance. And one may add in this context: the innocent civilians in Lebanon who lost their lives due to the Israeli raids are no less sacrificial rams; their blood is still calling from the ground and receives no answer.

As in previously discussed poems, thematic deflection is evident here, for the war in Lebanon is indirectly presented through the isolating screen of the *aqedah* fable. Consequently, an aesthetic distance is achieved and the poem is redeemed from potential sentimentality. "The Real Hero" is ironical, hyperbolic, and critically piercing. Shakespeare cleverly stated in Henry IV, "The arms are fair / When the intent of bearing them is just" (5.2.88-89). Indeed, despite questionable nature of the Lebanon conflict, Israel did not say farewell to fair arms. Long years of haunting attacks have produced a just intent for bearing arms, yet too many aspects of this continuing war are not fair. This change in the nature of war has dictated a change in Amichai's literary response to the subject. Though lamentation for the dead is undiminished, it is joined with biting irony and piercing criticism. In Amichai's verse, historical dynamics are faithfully shadowed by poetic dynamics. In this regard, his poetry aspires not only to mirror history but to judge it as well. Amichai's "war poem" is a "correct poem" not only because it extinguishes sentimentality and prefers a whisper to a cry, but also because it is a farewell to arms as much as it is a farewell to sentimentality.

A Pearl Under a Pile of Dust

Unearthing a Cryptic Appeal in the Poetry of Yehuda Amichai

Don't Tell Me I am Late The Separation Theme in Two Poems by Yehuda Amichai

"Late in my life I return to you
Filtered through many doors,
Sifted through stains,
Almost nothing is left of me"
—Yehuda Amichai, *Time*

The theme of separation is one of the most prominent, paramount themes in the comprehensive volume of Yehuda Amichai's poetry. In one of the lyrical sonnets, clustered under the title "We Loved Here", the narrator states while amalgamating both piercing sadness and mute, submissive acceptance: "But something, we knew, will never return—a boat, us, an echo of another world". In the poem "when a man comes to a certain place" (in *Now with Noise*), the withdrawn narrator gloomily confesses: "The last hand-shake of "welcome" / is the first hand-shake of separation". And later on, with subtle irony that metamorphosizes into sardonic sarcasm: "I am invited in life. But / I see that my hosts display signs of / Fatigue and impatience" ("I am Invited in life", in: *Behind all of that a Great Happiness is Hiding*). And the following line: "Farewell my face and your face is already a memory" ("Farewell" in : *Poems 1948-1962*).

Even Amichai's poems that display a carefully calculated effort to dim and numb the pain emerged by separation, to bridle the aching emotions, to dam the trail that may lead to undesirable pathetic sentimentality—they still cannot conceal the piercing pain that penetrates all kinds of separation.

Numerous kinds of separation populate the poetry of Yehuda Amichai: separation from a shielding, sheltering father; separation from the soothing refuge of the sweet memories of the past, of childhood, of youth; separation from a beloved woman who keeps haunting and tormenting his agonized recollection, stabbing them mercilessly like a myriad scalding scars; separation from a close, dear friend who got killed in brutal battle; separation from the sweet, tender touch of innocence; separation from the dreams, hopes, aspirations, and expectations that were rooted and inlaid in his distant past, never to be either materialized or resurrected. Separating himself from himself.

> *"What is it? It is an old warehouse filled with tools*
> *No, it is great love that has gone".*
>
> —Yehuda Amichai, *Time*

Both of Us Walked Together

Both of us walked together, like Abraham and Isaac.
You and I, We were a man and a woman
And we didn't go to aqeda. But also in our case
The knowledge of what will happen
with the lack of knowledge
Were attached to each other like lovers.

Later, jaws of suitcases opened wide
But what we assumed that will be only
for a few days of
Separation, had proven to be for good.

But since then have been left between us
Like signs given by
Two people who have never known each other
To meet in a place
Where they have never been before.

Aqeda means "binding" in Hebrew. The Biblical story (Genesis, 22) tells of God putting Abraham to the most devastating test of faith by commanding Abraham to bind to the altar his beloved son Isaac and sacrifice him as a burnt offering.

The entire situation depicted in this poem, its entire plot that is gradually unfolding, is founded on the theme of separation. Indeed, the poem's narrator mentions directly, clearly, a terminal separation. The reference to the suitcases is most certainly a very evident metonym to travel, one which is clearly engaged with separation. The fact that the open suitcases are metaphorically portrayed as jaws, ready to swallow, to consume the prey, further fortifies the idea of termination, which is the very vertex of terminal separation.

The first line of the poem—"Both of us walked together, like Abraham and Isaac"—evokes connotations of the most atrocious, horrendous separation to which God dooms Abraham and his beloved son, Isaac. No separation can be me more total, more hopeless than that morbid, deadly, mortal separation. But here the unfolding text plausibly displays its dynamic, vibrant, vital nature. After the text urged and goaded its reader to cultivate and nourish a certain kind of understanding (the separation is total, hopeless, morbid, deadly) a new, dramatically different situation is introduced: "like Abraham and Isaac." Hence, although initially it seems that Abraham and Isaac "walked together towards total, mortal separation, eventually their separation was avoided and they were reunited.

This is the way the dynamic mechanism of the textual continuum operates. In its first stage, the textual sequence provides information that instructs and encourages the reader to cultivate and adopt a certain kind of understanding. However, the following textual continuum unveils new information that sheds new light on the earlier information. This way, the reader is compelled to practice "reverse reading"—to reread the early information and reevaluate it according to the new light that the later information sheds upon it. In many cases, the new information just joins the earlier information. It may make the earlier information more detailed, more specific, but it does not change the way it was understood in its original, early placement in the textual continuum.

In other cases, however, the new light which the later information casts on the earlier one, does change moderately the previous understanding of the early information. Most certainly, in this case, the reader is compelled to practice "reverse" reading: he/she returns to the early information, reevaluates it according to the new light that is shed upon it by the later information and updates his/her early understanding accordingly.

The third type of dynamics of the text is the most drastic, dramatic one. In this case, the new light shed by the late information on the early information challenges and contradicts dramatically the early understanding, the one that was conceived and yielded by the early information. Again, the reader practices "reverse" reading, returns to the early information, but this time deletes and destroys entirely his/her early understanding, and replaces it with a completely new one, the one which is "inspired" and dictated by information which is later introduced along the textual continuum. This very drastic type of textual dynamics is the one that is employed and practiced in the poem "Both of Us Walked Together."

Hence, the first line of the poem ("Both of us walked together, like Abraham and Isaac") simultaneously contains the polar, contradictory, oscillating textual dynamics: separation and unification. The second line introduces the two persons who act on the stage of the poem: "You and I. We were a man and a woman." Not father and son who love each other but a man and a woman who are (probably) in love. And they did not go to aqeda. Since—as previously argued—the aqeda does not yield connotations of separation (as initially believed) the fact that the man and the woman, the male narrator and his female beloved, did not face separation.

Nevertheless, the textual dynamic swings again: "The knowledge of what will happen with the lack of knowledge" "The knowledge of what will happen" is Abraham's, who does not know that it is nothing but a test (only the reader knows that so his/her mind will be freed from worry and he/she will be able to pay full attention to Abraham and not to the thriller-like aspects of the story) so he/she is the one who possesses the knowledge, and Isaac is the one who is devoid of knowledge.

The latter swings back the oscillating pendulum (from separation to unification and vice versa) as the theme of separation revives Abraham's knowledge; his knowledge that by sacrificing his son, his beloved son, Isaac, the separation between them will be a brutal, total, eternal separation. What makes even further complicated is that Abraham—and not only Isaac—is also devoid of knowledge: he does not know that God's atrocious command is nothing but a test and Isaac will not be sacrificed after all.

The second consecutive stanza freezes and petrifies the oscillating pendulum in the separation pole: "Later, jaws of suitcases opened wide / And what we assumed that will be for a few days only of separation, had be found to be for good."

Suitcases are a natural metonym for travel a long distance, for a very long period of time. The open suitcase demonstrates packing for a very long voyage that dictates a very long separation, and portraying metaphorically the wide-open suitcases as “jaws” clearly echoes the wide open jaws of a beast of prey that is about to devour wildly its innocent, hopeless, helpless prey. No separation of the male lover from his female beloved can be portrayed in a more immense, blatantly brutal, heart-breaking fashion.

“*Sic transit Gloria mundi.*” The glory of the world evaporates, fades away, leaving nothing but “dust and ashes.” You came from soil and you will return to soil. Once you are gone, there is no way to return. The surf of the ocean, the surf of your life, will wilt in a blink of an eye: your memories, your ill-doings, your hopes, your failures, your lofty accomplishments, your piercing mis-takes, your humiliation, your shame, your ascending aspirations, your cultivating expectations.

All will be gone, nothing will be left. From dust to dust, from ashes to ashes. Even your good deeds in this world, on this scalding sois, will be forsaken, forgotten, sooner or later. What will be left is the vertex of nothingness. Even your name, dexterously engraved on your tombstone, will fade, will be erased by moss, wind, and rain will wither through the passing years.

“*Tempus edax rerum.*” Time consumes / devours all things. Ironically, separation is the only sure thing in human’s life. It may occur early. It may occur late. But it always occurs.

> *“Vanity of vanities, said Koheleth, vanity of vanities, all is vanity” (Ecclesiastes 1;2)*

Indeed, suitcases are metonyms for travel, which is a metonym for separation. But separation can end and eventually turns into nothingness. In light of this, the separation-unification pendulum quits oscillating, freezes between the two contradictory poles, while leaving the reader waiting anxiously for the continuation, one that will determine which pole prevails and which pole is "muted." And that eagerly expected continuation is introduced with no delay:

> *"And what we believed that will be for a few days*
> *only of separation, had he found to be for good."*

Hence the oscillating pendulum eventually rests on the total separation pole, solidly cemented to it without leaving room for even a sliver of frail, faint hope.

> *"But since then have been left between us*
> *Like signs given by*
> *Two people who have never known each other*
> *To meet in a place*
> *Where they have never before."*

In *prima vista*, at first glance, it seems that perhaps, after all, a tiny, minute crack opens in the dam of separation; this stanza mentions signs that will enable people to meet, to practice unification. After the pole of separation prevailed vigorously, the opposite pole, the pole of unification, of togetherness is resurrected, is revived. But the latter could not be more misleading. That unification is an idle one, a vain one. This third, last stanza of the poem, commences with the following statement which is a sort of a promise: "But since then have been left between us." Yet, that promise is breached, is never fulfilled; the stanza fails to tell what have been left between the narrator and his female beloved. The stanza fails to tell what have been left because nothing has been left. Nothing.

Hence that unification is nothing but a hoax, a promise that is doomed to be denied, sentenced to be frustrated. The oscillation between the two conflicting poles has reached its total termination. The oscillating riddle has nested in the separation pole and moved no more. The unification pole has been abandoned, muted.

Indeed, this is a poem about separation. Only separation. Introducing the desirable pole, the pole of unification, as well as the oscillation between the pole of unification and the pole of separation is nothing but a camouflage: it goads and urges the reader to cultivate optimistic expectations (the separation will not materialize after all) only in order to breach and frustrate them. This way the separation is introduced in the most bleak, murky fashion. Somber and dismal is the separation. And no unification is looming on the distant, misty horizon.

When the Past Turns into a Dusky, Sooty Dust
The People on this Beach

The people on this beach will never
Mint again their footprints in the
Footsteps which they left behind them.

This is a weeping truth
But sometimes it weeps out of happiness
Because the world is large, and there is no need
To go back in it. Everything is inside heavens.

At dusk time I saw a sun-tanned life-guard
Bending over a golden-tanned drowned woman
To respire her with his mouth, like lovers kissing.

The people on this beach will never
Mint again their footprints in the
Footsteps which they left behind them.

That statement is simultaneously false and valid. Practically, it is false. Hence, people can mint again their footprints which they left behind them while strolling along the beach. Hence, practically it is very doable indeed. However, behind that valid, doable practicality, another layer of meaning can be unearthed. That "cryptic" layer is both truthful and philosophical "lesson" can be unveiled by deciphering its metaphorical substance.

Also in this poem one can trace a dynamic oscillation process in which a later statement contradicts the previous one. In such a case, the reader is compelled to practice "reverse reading": to reread the earlier text and update his/her previous understanding of that early text in light of the newly introduced information. Sometimes the updating process is moderate, but in many cases, the updating process is drastic. Accordingly, the previous, early understanding is proven to be totally wrong. Thus, it must be deleted and replaced with a completely new understanding, one that is dictated by the new information that is unearthed in a more advanced stage of the textual sequence.

The textual dynamics in this poem materialize (at least partially, not along the entire textual continuum) quite differently. The first stanza consists of a structure of a metaphor in which two components reciprocally interact; the tenor and the vehicle (two terms coined by I.A. Richard's terms, in "metaphor", in his *The Philosophy of Thetoric*, N.Y., 1938, pp. 87-138). The tenor is the "semantic bedrock" of the metaphor, its latent substance, its cryptic thematic meaning and the vehicle is the "modifier," the image that portrays and conveys the latent, thematic meaning of the metaphor.

The reciprocal interaction between the tenor and the vehicle, the active dialogue between the two components of the metaphor, the vehicle and the tenor, do yield a specific case of textual dynamics, of the way early information and late information reciprocally relate to each other along the textual sequence, when the reader encounters the poem's first stanza, does he/she encounter the vehicle (which is factually false). Practically, it is possible to mint again the footprints in previously minted footsteps. That falsehood operates in the capacity of a trigger that ignites the reader's curiosity, one that leads him to unveil the "cryptic" tenor, which is of a philosophical/existential meaning: there is no way to revive the past, to resurrect the past.

As it is poetically formulated in one of the most powerful, enticing Jewish prayers; "a withering twig, a wilting bud, wind blew through it and it is gone." Undoubtedly, the transition from the vehicle to the tenor, from falsehood to profound philosophical, existential meaning, is conditioned by textual dynamics, by a transformation from an "earthly" "phase" to a philosophical, existential one.

> *"This is a weeping truth*
> *But sometimes it weeps out of happiness*
> *Because the world is large, and there is no need*
> *To go back in it. Everything is inside heavens."*

In this second stanza of the poem, the "traditional" textual continuum/sequence is "resurrected," is "revived." Indeed, the first line ("This is a weeping truth") echoes the first stanza, the one that mourns and laments the wailing that there is no way to repeat the past, to correct and cure the past. "*Tempus edax rerum*" heralds the Latin adage: Time devours everything, nothing of the past is left; the past is beyond our reach, the trail left by the past consists of nothingness.

"*ILL fatt-maat*" says the Arabic adage: "Whatever happened in the past—is dead." At this point of despair, however, the pendulum of the textual dynamics, the sequential, progressive nature of the text, swings again, oscillates again. The bleak, murky character of the second stanza's first line ("This is a weeping truth") unexpectedly converts into a happy one in the consecutive, second line: "But sometimes it [the weeping truth] weeps out of happiness."

The following third line and part of the fourth line, provide the reason for that unforeseen happiness: "Because the world is large, and there is no need/To go back in it." Hence, through the textual dynamics, through the textual oscillation, the somber "philosophy" is not only replaced by a blissful one, but also the reason for that felicitous metamorphosis is provided. That metamorphosis is followed by the consequential statement:

> *"Everything is inside heavens."*

The enigmatic nature of that statement is clarified once one realizes that it alludes to the following Hebrew/Jewish adage: *"Ha-Kol Bidey Shamayim,"* "Everything is in the hands of Heavens."

As previously noted, the last oscillation rests on the positive pole: the world is large, there is no need to go back in it and therefore not going back in the world is truth that weeps out of happiness, of bliss. However, the original Hebrew/Jewish adage—"everything is in the hands of heavens"—pulls the oscillating riddle from the positive pole to the negative pole by practicing reverse textual continuum. Accordingly, if everything is in the hands of heavens (God), it means that human beings are devoid of the capacity to navigate freely their lives and they are doomed and sentenced to destiny, which is forced upon them while damming and muting their free will. For that very reason the poem's narrator deviates from the original Hebrew/Jewish adage by deleting "in the hands of heavens" and replacing it with "inside heavens." This way, the positive oscillating momentum (the textual dynamics) is kept. The poem concludes with the following third stanza:

"At dusk I saw a sun-tanned life-guard
Bending over a golden-tanned drowned woman
To respire her with his mouth, like kissing lovers."

Although the depicted situation is tragic (a woman who drowned in the sea), the soft, mellow, balmy hues (dusk, sun-tanned, golden-tanned, as well as the appartent kissing between two seeming lovers) bestow upon the situation a tint of tender tranquility, even enticing serenity.

When it comes to the textual dynamics, to the accumulating momentum of the text, it seems that in this case, the oscillating riddle is fluctuating in a twilight zone between the two conflicting poles, the negative one and the positive one. Although the woman drowned (negative pole), there is an attempt to rescue her (positive pole). However, it is not certain that that revival attempt will meet success (a twilight path between the two conflicting poles). Hence, the poem that consists of oscillations between the negative pole and the positive pole, ends with a dead-end: the oscillating riddle is "caged" between the two conflicting polar options, snared between the two, devoid of its previous momentum.

What is the poem about? It is also a poem about separation: separation from the past that will never be revived, never be resurrected. And even the question mark that is introduced at the termination of the poem (will the drowned woman be revived?) does not leave much place for hope. After all, even the lovers in this concluding stanza, are not real lovers, are nothing but an opaque illusion. And the sunset hues that engulf the concluding stanza, are gentle harbingers that herald termination, separation. No doubt, the curtain is pulled down.

Indeed, Like a Natural Path in the Desert. Yet, Aesthetic Engineering in Yehuda Amichai's Poetry

In one of the interviews (with the Hebrew/Israeli poet Ronny Someck) Yehuda Amichai said—among other things—the following:

A poem should be as natural as a path in the desert. Not like a paved road that was compressed and asphalted by a heavy roller, designed fastidiously by landscape engineers. A natural path in the desert is treaded by wild animals according to their needs: closeness to brooks, to springs, to other sources of water, landscape which is a shielding shelter from beasts of prey, an orbit that provides shade in the scorching sun of the desert, a lane which is not too steep to climb up.

Indeed, that simile, the natural path in the desert simile, is the very best aesthetic ambassador of Yehuda Amichai's poetry. And even when Amichai's poetry displays aesthetic intricacy, poetic complexity (shrewdly concealed by surface simplicity) it still does not give up the impression of natural fluency, of spontaneous flow, like a natural path in the desert.

When I was a Child

When I was a child
Tall grass and masts were towering on the sea shore
And I, while lying down there,
Failed to tell the difference between them
Since they all ascended to the sky above me.
Only my mother's words were with me
Like a slice of bread wrapped with rustle paper
And I did not know when my father will return
As there was another forest beyond the
forest's clearing.

Everything stretched a hand,
A bull gored the sun with its horns,
And at nights the light of the streets caressed
My cheeks and the walls,
And the moon, like a big jug, lowered itself
And quenched my thirsty slumber.

The poem consists of two stanzas, and an immediate question surfaces; what is the aesthetic rationale for that structural bisection? As will be further plausibly argued, that structural bisection is neither random nor arbitrary as it reflects the very essence of the poem's meaning.

The first stanza adopts and cultivates the child's perspective. While lying down on the ground, not far away from the seashore, he observes the boats' masts and the grass' stalks. Yet, he fails to tell the difference between them as all of them ascended high above, over his head.

The failure to tell the difference between masts of boats and stalks of grass does attest to a childish perspective.

However, that image tells the reader much more than that. That image tells the reader how lonely the child is. Both his mother and his father are far away and there is neither knowledge nor certainty when (or even if) they will return. Only his mother's words escort him "Like a slice of bread wrapped with rustle paper." That image brings to mind a sandwich, which is a clear metonym of travel, of going away. The father is also connected with being away: "And I did not know when my father will return as there was another forest beyond the forest's clearing."

The dense thicket of the forest is connected with going astray, with erring, with losing one's way. Thus the separation from the father, the one which is engaged with a forest, turns both disheartening and threatening. The fact that there is a forest's clearing provides neither comfort nor relief "As there was another forest beyond the forest's clearing."

Hence, the child does not feel only lonely: he feels forsaken, deserted, abandoned, neglected. No wonder that the child, who is snared in his menacing loneliness, who is besieged by his engulfing solitude, is looking for a soothing comfort, for a shielding shelter. That soothing comfort, that shielding shelter, can be provided by a dream only.

And the poem's second stanza provides that dream. That is the very reason for the poem's structural bisection into two separate stanzas: while the first stanza introduces somber distance in reality, one that desperately seeks soothing comfort, the second stanza introduces a dream that acts in the capacity of that desirable, soothing comfort. Hence, only in a dream all desirable wishes can materialize, only in a balmy, emollient dream, the suffocating reality can meet its pacifying comfort. For a limited period of time, at least, until the dream evaporates. Fades away, until the dream encounters its termination, and the thorny, stabbing reality, reintroduces itself.

Indeed, the dream functions as a comforting, soothing dream should function; it is saturated with serene atmosphere of softness, tenderness, gentleness. "Everything stretched a hand" to touch the child compassionately, gracefully; the nocturnal, mellow, agreeable light caresses mercifully the houses' walls and the child's cheeks; "and the moon, like a big jug, lowered itself/ And quenched my [the child's] thirsty slumber."

On the face of it, the image of a bull that "gored" the sun with its horns" seems to upset the dream's pastoral, serene, soft atmosphere. However, the bull gores with its horns the sun that radiates scorching, scalding, blinding light, which violates the atmosphere of soft, tender, mellow serenity of the dream. Hence, also the bull, which gores the sun with its horns, is part of the tender, touching, docile atmosphere of the dream.

This way, the second stanza compensates for the acute lack of the first stanza. Indeed, the dream (like all dreams) cannot remedy the child's distress in the first stanza: he seems to be sentenced to his blatantly desperate loneliness. Yet, the dream redeems him for a while from his biting tribulation. And under such circumstances of consuming anguish, even a brief relief is cherished.

By An Archaeological Excavation

By an archaeological excavation I saw pieces
of broken clay
Which are precious, well washed, cleaned
and pampered.
And I saw next to them a heap of poured dust
Which is worthless for growing even
thistles and thorns.

I asked: what is this dust that was tested
That was hurled, that was tormented and later
Was poured? And I said to myself: this dust
Is people like us who were separated in their lives
From copper, from gold and from marble,
as well as in their death.
This dust is us, our bodies and our souls,
All the words in our mouths, all our hopes.

The situation in the poem is clear: the poem's speaker is facing an archaeological excavation. He sees "pieces of broken clay / Which are precious, well washed, cleaned and pampered". Naturally, those pieces (finds of the archeological excavation) of broken clay are the very vertex of the archaeological excavation. Yet, the speaker focuses on the worthless dust that previously covered those broken pieces of clay:

> *"And I saw next to them a heap of poured dust which is worthless for growing even thistles and thorns."*

The heap of the worthless dust alludes to the well known Biblical verse that attests to the mortality of human beings: "For dust you are and to dust you shall return" (Genesis 3:19). The focus of the poem's speaker on the marginal dust, and not on the valuable archaeological finds (the pieces of broken clay) is meaningful. It ignites a Biblical allusion to the prophet Ezekiel and his dry bones prophetic vision. The allusion to Ezekiel's dry bones prophetic vision materializes on three levels.

First, the allusion is on materialistic level: the heap of the dry dust in the poem echoes the heap of the dry bones, amassed in the vale, in Ezekiel's dry bones prophetic vision.

Second, the situation in both compound cases is the same. In both cases, facing the heap of the dry dust/ bones, kindles meditation about the destiny of mortal human beings.

Third, the analogy between Amichai's poem in focus and Ezekiel's prophetic vision of the dry bones, is also rhetorical: both are conveyed through a dialogue. In the case of Ezekiel, the dialogue is between God and the prophet. "He [God] said to men, oh mortal, can these bones live again? And I replied, oh, Lord God, only You know" (Ezekiel 37:3). In the case of Amichai's poem, the dialogue is an internal dialogue between the speaker and himself ("I asked...And I said...") The closeness between Amichai's poem in focus and Ezekiel's prophetic vision of the dry bones is further fortified as the poem's speaker says the following:

> *"This dust is us, our bodies and our souls,*
> *All the words in our mouths, all our hopes".*

And such are the dead, dry bones in Ezekiel's prophetic vision.

That and more. Portraying the dust in the poem as "tormented" further reinforces its analogy to people in the poem, as well as to the dead people (the dry bones) in Ezekiel's prophetic vision. The somber destiny of the dust of the people who will never be resurrected is further emphasized by the fact that while it is tormented, the pieces of broken clay "are precious, well washed, cleaned and pampered." That and more. While the dead people (the dry bones) in Ezekiel's prophetic vision will be resurrected, the dead people in the poem (the dust) are doomed to eternal mortality. And the speaker is the only living soul who mourns and laments their death.

More About Artistic Dexterity in Yehuda Amichai's Poetry

Portrait of Sadness as a One-Way Travel Ticket

The poem: "People Travel a Great Distance"

Like many poems by Yehuda Amichai, this poem also surrenders an impression of elementary simplicity. As Sherlock Holmes put it: "Elementary, Watson, elementary." Yet, the *prima vista* of the poem, the one that unleashes such a first response to the poem, is found most misleading indeed. Like a title of Amichai's volume of poetry, *Behind all of that Great Happiness is Concealed*," in this poem behind the surface simplicity, great aesthetic intricacy is concealed. Hence, a more observant, analytical look at the poem unearths a latent level of aesthetic sophistication.

People Travel a Great Distance

People travel great distances only to
Say: "It reminds me of another place.
It feels like then, it is similar. "But
I have known a man who traveled to New York
To commit suicide. He argued that the houses in
Jerusalem
Are too low and also people know him.

I remember him favorably, as he asked me to leave
The classroom, in the middle of the lesson, saying:
"A beautiful woman is waiting for you outside, in the garden."
And he calmed down the noisy children...

When I think about the woman and the garden,
I remember him on the high roof, about
The loneliness of his death and the death of his loneliness.

The poem commences with the following statement:

"People travel great distances only to
say: It reminds me of another place,"

"It feels like then, it is similar." This statement reflects an ironical, critical paradox: what is the point in traveling great distances if the final destination of such travels echoes their starting point? It is like traveling in a closed circle that takes the travelers to nothing, that leads the travelers to nothing. It is a travel to nowhere, a travel that its ending is doomed from it very beginning, that is sentenced to nothingness from its very commencement. The travel is a vain one, an idle one, a pointless one: The great distance is nothing but a geographical illusion that leads astray. That travel leads to a dead-end.

"But I have known a man who traveled to New York
To commit suicide there. He argued that the houses in Jerusalem
Are too low and also people know him."

Also this travel leads to a dead-end. To the dead-morbid-end of the traveler. Hence, under the surface of the two images, one can unearth a solid, robust bond: a travel to a dead-end, a travel to a destination that does not exist, a travel to the very vertex of nothingness. Despite the surface, "epidermic" difference between the two images, the inner analogy between them is firmly fortified.

> *"I remember him favorably, as he asked me to leave the classroom in a middle of a lesson, saying: 'A beautiful woman is waiting for you, in the garden' And he calmed down the noisy children..."*

A careful scrutiny of this stanza traces the following three elements, which are reciprocally connected on grounds of an allusion: the beautiful woman, the garden (in Hebrew: *gan)* and the teacher (an autocratic figure). Each of those three elements, while being introduced separately, seems to be devoid of substance in the context of the poem. However, once the three of them are clustered together, they produce a meaning that echoes the meaning of the first stanza, which is indeed the meaning of the entire poem.

In the story of the Garden of Eden, in the book of Genesis, the Garden of Eden is called *gan* (garden; Genesis, 3:2; "you should not eat the fruit of the tree in the *gan*/garden"). The beautiful woman in the garden, in the *gan*, may bring to mind Eve in the *gan* of Eden and the teacher, the man of authority (who "calms down the noisy children") may stand for God, the figure absolute, supreme authority. This way, the amalgamation of the *gan*, the beautiful woman, and the figure of great authority seem to echo Adam and Eve in the Garden of Eden while being evicted by God (the figure of absolute, supreme authority) from the *gan*, the Garden of Eden for good, until encountering their mortality. Hence, the second stanza as well enlists metaphors for a travel, which ends with a mortal destination. The dead-end destination in the commencement of the poem turns into a terminal one, into a deadly one, into loss of both innocence and mortality.

> *"When I think about the woman and the garden,*
> *I remember him on the high roof*
> *The loneliness of his death and the death of his loneliness."*

The last, concluding stanza of the poem, clusters together all the previously introduced components, which are engaged with vain, worthless travel that leads to the point of departure; with travel to New York, which is a mortal travel to death; and the eviction from the Garden of Eden, which is eviction from immortality, eviction to deadly dust, to the land of the dead. And each mortal travel: the travel that eventually brings us to the point of departure, the deadly travel to commit suicide in New York, and the deadly travel away from the immortality of the Garden of Eden.

All those terminal, mortal travels yield bleak, murky, somber loneliness. And the deadly loneliness, and the loneliness of the death of that person who throws himself from the roof of a high building in New York, is the very venomous vertex of that dismal, dim, doleful loneliness. And there is not even a sliver of redemption or salvation.

"For dust you are and to dust you shall return" (Genesis, 3:19)

"Ever turning blows the wind, or its rounds the wind returns" (Ecclesiastes 7:6).

The terminal outcome of travel is already doomed before it was launched. Portrait of human life as a somber circle, as a desolate snare from which there is no way out. A travel that leads to the starting point of nothingness, a travel the launching point is bitter bararess.

SOMBER AESTHETICS THREE HOLOCAUST POEMS BY YEHUDA AMICHAI

BUONA NOTTE, OUR MUTE LORD, NEVER *ARRIVEDERCI* YOUR MURDERED NATION:

The Poem: "The Synagogue in Florence"

In these days, God leaves the earth
And retires to His summer manor
In the dark hills...
And leaves us with scalding winds, wickedness and slaughter.

—Yehuda Amichai,
from "*Beginning of the Summer*"

This skillfully sculpted poem is one that plausibly displays subtle aesthetic intricacy as well as a roaring, outraged message. It is a message that aims at the beasts who orchestrated and executed the Holocaust, as well as at God, who turned mute and became paralyzed during the Holocaust. Like the previously discussed Holocaust poem by Fogel, it is a poem that represents a marginal, yet still powerful, minority in the gigantic, comprehensive volume of Amichai's poetry. Equally cogent, this poem acts as an ambassador of his glowing greatness as a poet.

The vital evidence to that worthy aesthetic intricacy represented by Amichai's poem in focus (as well as by numerous poems of his that reach an artistic zenith) consists of the following. Although it is a Holocaust poem, it does not surrender its true nature until it reaches its very zenith, at its terminating accord. Hence, throughout the accumulated, verbal sequence of the poem, the poem's narrator dedicatedly spreads subtle hints of a certain deadly cloud that hovers over the silent serenity, over the innocent play of four girls and the enticing scent of the blossoming tree.

Only at the very end of the poem, however, does the reader realize that all those slowly accumulated hints – those that relate to a certain opaque calamity – practically address the Holocaust. In this way, the literary dynamics of the poem are cleverly cultivated into one that consists of the sequential character of the text and is part of the poem's handsomely rewarding aesthetic virtues. All of the above, and much more, shall be discussed after introducing the poem in English translation.

Your Murdered Nation

The Poem: The Synagogue in Florence

Softness of spring in the backyard
A blossoming tree, four girls are playing
During the recess between two classes of
the holy language
In front of a memorial wall made of marble:
Levy, Sorino, Casouto and others
In straight lines like in a newspaper
Or in the Bible.

And the tree stands in memory of nothing,
Only in memory of this spring,
Arrivederci, our Father
Buona Notte, our King.

Tears in the eyes
Like dry crumbs in the pocket,
From a cake that existed once.

Buona Notte Sorino
Arrivederci, the six million,
The girls and the tree and the crumbs.

The first stanza opens upon an idyllic scene of peaceful innocence (the four girls who are playing serenely), the scented blossoming of a budding tree, and the feathery softness of spring. The reference to classes dedicated to the holy language, Hebrew, further fortifies the atmosphere of pacified calmness, while adding an aspect of tranquil spirituality.

Nevertheless, the first ripple in that enticingly pleasing, quiescent atmosphere manifests itself once the reader is notified that the charming, enticingly captivating scene, including the innocent play of the four girls, takes place in front of a memorial wall (or plaque) that announces the names of the dead-"In straight lines like in a newspaper/ Or in the Bible." The list of the names cannot be connected yet to the dead in the Holocaust. At this early point of the poem's initial unfolding, there is no valid evidence that may allude to any connection whatsoever between the synagogue's wall that declares the Jewish community's dead and the Holocaust's dead.

The latter is further reinforced due to the fact such a memorial wall/plaque is very common in every synagogue and is equally so in churches as well. Nevertheless, at the very ending of the poem, the connection between the list of the dead on the synagogue's wall/plaque and the Holocaust will be unveiled. A new, elucidating light will be shed on the beginning of the poem (or most of it). It will force readers to practice a revers reading, to reread the poem in order to update and correct the way they previously understood the poem's commencement and responded to it.

The narrator describes the way the names of the dead are engraved on the memorial wall/plaque: "In straight lines like in a newspaper/ Or in the Bible." Such a description is amazingly surprising on grounds of both theme and composition. In terms of theme, portraying the lines of the names of the dead like lines in the Bible calls for a stupendous respect and surrenders a tint of eternity. However, at the same time, the Bible's sacred lines are being compared to lines in a newspaper. This stands for a daily, ephemeral, mundane existence-a newspaper that reports, among other things, the sewage flood, crime, and alcoholism; a newspaper that advertises shampoo and tampons; a newspaper that tomorrow will be worthless and used for wrapping fish in the market. Such a comparison between lines in the Bible and lines in a daily, cruddy, cheap, withering newspaper is outrageously offensive. It despises the sacred memory of the dead, as well as mocks the Bible's holiness.

Although the compositional surprise is not as staggering as the thematic surprise, it is certainly shocking as well. The egregious, flagrant comparison between the lines in the Bible and a shoddy newspaper's lines, whose relevance fades and withers in less than a day (thematic device), is compositionally organized along the poem's textual continuum, in the most astounding fashion. Accordingly, upon outrageously comparing the Bible to a cheap, ephemeral newspaper (the thematic device), the newspaper comes first while the Bible comes second (that means last). This is a compositional device since the composition is in charge of placing the thematic material (Bible, dead, memorial wall, tree, newspaper, lines, girls, spring, synagogue, marble, and more, in the case of this poem) along the textual sequence.

Most certainly, placing the newspaper prior to the Bible (compositional device) mobilizes and utilizes the sequential, accumulative nature of the textual continuum. This is done to further reinforce the astounding comparison between the Bible and a newspaper. However, only at the very end-at the very somber vertex of the poem, the one that introduces clearly and plausibly the Holocaust as the poem's true topic-will the reader comprehend the aesthetic purpose that drives and propels the astonishing comparison between the Bible and a newspaper.

Accordingly, that comparison (that consists of a rhetorical device, since it is rhetoric that dictates the literary text's impact on the reader, as well as molding and conditioning the reader's response to the literary text) aims to dilute and attenuate the acid, mordant, morbid impact of the Holocaust's atrocities. Otherwise, such a device could create a shocking impact that would translate into tasteless sentimentality. This would flood the text while drowning its worthy qualities. An aesthetic mission to counter this is accomplished by associating analogously the holy with the mundane. Through this, the holy is hurt, becomes polluted, defiled, infected, and befouled. Correspondingly, the dose of holiness descends and degenerates, which helps to avoid and evict sentimentality. This is crucial in a Holocaust poem where extreme feelings must be restrained and tempered in order to maintain an emotional balance.

Only at the apex of the poem, when readers realize that the poem in focus deals with the Holocaust, do they comprehend to the fullest the aesthetic purpose that yields, guides, and leads the performance of that remarkably questionable comparison between the newspaper and the Bible: it does not operate to offend the reader, neither to pay disrespect to the Bible, but rather to protect the poem's aesthetic worthiness by avoiding over-emotionality and exiling sentimentality from the realms of the poem. Hence, upon reaching the end of the poem, the reader will appreciate increasingly how the poem cleverly uses the verbal medium, by dexterously practicing the sequential continuum character of the text.

The second stanza unfolds as follows:

And the tree stands in memory of nothing,
Only in memory of this spring,
Arrivederci, our Father
Buona Notte, our King.

Undoubtedly, this stanza makes progress towards unveiling the evil of the Holocaust, which is the latent, true topic of this poem. Accordingly, this very stanza is heavily saturated with thematic (adjective form of theme, which stands for semantic unit[s]) materials. All of them, simultaneously, express blatantly bitter, scorching, acid accusation against the indifference (later it will be found out that that cold indifference was practiced by God during the Holocaust) that watched calmly the atrocities while displaying a heartless, uncaring attitude: "And the tree stands in memory of nothing." Traditionally, a tree is planted in memory of the dead, notably when its location is near a memorial wall. Here, however, the tree ignores, denies, and contests its mission to commemorate the dead (stressed by its location near the memorial wall/plaque) and indulges itself with the soft scent of the blossoming spring.

The concluding two lines of the second stanza increase the dose of the bitterly blatant accusation by aiming it at

God himself, while enlisting the most acid, sarcastic, sardonic irony:

Arrivederci, our Father
Buona Notte, our King.

That poetic pattern is adopted from the well-known Jewish prayer, *Avinu Malkenu*, our Father, our King (which relates to God as Father and King). Among the phrases of this prayer, one reads the following:

Our Father, our King, we have sinned against You.
Our Father, our King, we have no King but You.
Our Father, our King, help us because of
Your merciful nature.
Our Father, Our King, forgive and pardon all our sins.
Our Father, our King, remember us with favor.

That Jewish prayer, relates to God as a father and a king, who with his mercy, compassion, loving kindness, and generosity not only protects, shields, and shelters His chosen people, but equally forgives them for their sins, transgressions, and iniquities.

The ending of the second stanza, however, unfolds the following:

Arrivederci, our Father
Buona Notte, our King.

Arrivederci, our Father? Farewell, our Father? Are you leaving? Have not you already left? We shall no longer enjoy your mercy and protection? And what does it mean,

Buona Notte, our King, Good Night, our King? Is it time for you to retire to your royal chambers, to your bedroom and go to sleep? Is it time on your part, our father, our king, to say so long to us, to fall asleep, to pamper yourself with sweet dreams while we are oppressed, tormented, raped, abused, murdered, strangled, our skulls crushed to the wall, our infants buried alive, stoned, burnt, and butchered?

Hence the ending of the second stanza utilizes the famous Jewish prayer, only to distort both ironically and sarcastically its original nature. It is used to scold God—sharply and scornfully—for His indifferent muteness during the Holocaust, to contest, challenge and demolish His reputation as a father, a king of mercy.

Indeed, the Holocaust is not mentioned. Yet clearly, it is unveiled in an openly macabre fashion, at the very vertex and end of the poem. However, the context of the poem, that part now unearthed gives license to assume that the Holocaust is the poem's cornerstone, its prominent topic. The bleak, murky ending of the poem proves that solid, sound assumption to be persuasively valid.

The third stanza continues the leading trend of unearthing the poem's somber topic, one that eventually will be found to be the Holocaust:

Tears in the eyes
Like dry crumbs in the pocket
From the cake that existed once.

The tears in the eyes are the very first manifestation in the poem that attests to a somber, bleak, dark experience, to sadness that continues to piercingly penetrate the hurting heart.

Hence, so many floods of tears had been overflowing to the point that they had left dry the wells of weeping, mourning lamenting. Accordingly, the tears had metamorphosed into dry, withered crumbs of a cake that does not exist any more. The fact that those lifeless crumbs are "in the pocket," alludes validly to the plausibility that those dead cake's crumbs are in a pocket of a child. It is much more likely that a child, and not an adult, will carry a piece of cake in his/her pocket.

On the other hand, however, the idea that a person carries cake in his/her pocket brings to mind the Holocaust. In order to increase their chances of survival, the victims carried, in their pockets, any possible leftover food. Maybe. Perhaps. Also here, God who already left ("Arrivederci, our Father"), who already went to sleep ("Buona Notte, our King"), is the same indifferent, merciless God, who had shut his mouth, ears, and eyes, when millions of His chosen people (and other millions of innocent people as well), were murdered, butchered, buried alive, suffocated with gas, thrown alive to the fire, their skulls smashed to the wall.

The fountain of the tears of the innocent, tormented, and slain victims had dried already, had turned arid, as dry as crumbs of cake that quit existing a long time ago. But God had not abandoned His heartless, merciless, indifference: He retired to His chambers, while getting ready to go to sleep ("Buona Notte, our King"); He had taken his departure ("Arrivederci, our Father"). Arrivederci? We'll see you? It is more than doubtful. And besides, where were you when we wanted, so desperately, to see you?

One of Amichai's powerful poems, one that also scolds God for merciless indifference, opens with the following words: "*El maleh rachamim*" (God full of mercy). This is a partial citation from the Jewish prayer for the dead. In the poem by Amichai, the narrator blames God for filling Himself with the entire reservoir of mercy, while leaving nothing for human beings. Such bitterly blatant blame is evidently relevant to the poem under discussion as well.

The poem in focus, however, concludes with the following stanza:

Buona Notte, Sorino
Arrivederci, the six million,
The girls and the tree and the crumbs.

Thus, the poem's concluding stanza formally unveils, for the very first time, the poem's cryptic topic (although it was gradually unveiled, through an accumulative momentum along the poem's textual continuum): "the six million..." Being the poem's final stanza, however, it is neither random nor arbitrary that this one is most exceedingly saturated with blatantly biting and bitter irony. That irony aims at God, who said "*Buona Notte*" (Good Night) when He should have been on guard and come to the rescue of the innocent millions of people (Jews and non-Jews), who did not have to say "*Arrivederci*" (Farewell) to those millions who needed badly his presence, not His nonchalant departing words.

This stanza opens with the following line: "Buona Notte, Sorino." Sorino is one of the names that is engraved on the synagogue's memorial wall/plaque. "Buona Notte, Sorino" sheds a sharper light on his death since the night (notte) is traditionally associated with death. The expression "Buona Notte" (Good Night) can be also associated—on grounds of connotations—with a compassionate, forbearing parent, who blesses tenderly, soothingly his/her child upon bedtime. The latter further reinforces the irony that is displayed by this line. Accordingly, neither tender, feathery softness, nor a truly good night are awaiting for Sorino, but rather a cold, deadly night, as wicked as a murderer who lurks in snaring, thorny ambush.

The last stanza's two concluding lines are no less scaldingly ironic:

Arrivederci, the six million,
The girls and the tree and the crumbs.

When one says "Arrivederci/Farewell/I'll see you," it is commonly considered a casual expression that means: "Well, so long, farewell for now, I'll see you in the near future." Correspondingly, using such a casual expression when addressing the tortured, torched innocent victims of the Holocaust (the girls as well? It is quite opaque) seems to befoul, defile, and soil the sacred memory of the Holocaust's victims. Neither 'arrivederci' for them, nor "see you": nobody will see them anymore.

Thus, using the expression "Arrivederci/I'll see you" upon approaching the Holocaust's innocent, tormented victims produces scalding, scolding irony, one that aims angrily at God: Arrivederci to the millions of butchered victims? We'll see you millions of victimized, helpless, hopeless people after you had been slain, suffocated, hung, stoned, butchered burnt alive, buried alive, and turned into ashes and dust? Where shall we see you? Where shall we meet your ashes and dust? In the heavenly, celestial kingdom, where God said to Himself "Buona Notte." Where He shut His eyes and sealed His heart when millions of you were yearning for His help, upon being butchered? Thus, one cannot imagine a more dense dose of blatantly biting, bitter, condemning irony. Squeezed into two tiny lines, it aims at God, on behalf of the millions whom He deserted as they were slain and slaughtered.

The very last line, however, may introduce wonder on behalf of the reader: "[Arrivederci] The girls and the tree and the crumbs." What is the common denominator that bonds the girls, the tree, and the crumbs in the context of the Holocaust? On the surface, they seem to be bonded randomly, arbitrarily. On the level of the poem's underlying currents, however, one may plausibly track a very evident connection among the three.

Accordingly, the girls, the tree, and the crumbs are metonyms for feelings, emotions, and characteristics of a world that had vanished, had been devastated, does not exist anymore. The girls are a metonym for innocence, the crumbs for the tears of sadness (see third stanza), and the tree is a metonym for loneliness (a lonely tree that grew next to a memorial wall). In this respect, the poem's concluding line abridges the very essence of the Holocaust: the innocence, the loneliness, the sadness of those who perished. Buona Notte to a post-Holocaust world. No arrivederci is waiting for you. And never will.

Throughout the analysis of the poem in focus, the literary mechanism that consists of the dynamics of the text has been mentioned frequently. One realizes that a cluster of foreshadowing hints to the Holocaust are planted along the poem's textual continuum. Those hints may be metaphorically compared with an embryo that while in its current stage of development is still far from being a human being (or an animal). Eventually, the embryo will complete its entire course of development, turning into a human being (or an animal).

Upon relating to the literary hints that are spread along the poem's textual sequence, they shall also unveil and reveal the hints' full identity (as literary ambassadors of the Holocaust) once the poem reaches its conclusion. Those early hints are as follows: the memorial wall/plaque that honors the dead; the innocence of the young girls that shall be cut off cruelly by the Holocaust (as happened to one and a half million Jewish children during the Holocaust); the lonely tree that stands in its somber solitude next to the memorial wall/plaque that commemorates the dead; the names of the dead on the memorial wall/plaque; relating to God in the context of the indifference of the tree that "stands in memory of nothing" while accusing God for being indifferent during the Holocaust; the dry tears like crumbs of a forgotten cake; the ironic, repeating words in Italian—"Buona Notte" (Good Night) and Arrivederci" (Farewell)—that blatantly, bitterly express the most piercing *j'accuse* against God, who left ("Arrivederci") and went to sleep ("Buona Notte") while the Holocaust went on, and millions of people—Jews and non-Jews—were slaughtered in the most brutal, beastly fashion. All those literary hints act metaphorically in the capacity of embryos that will reach their full evolution at the end of the poem, unveiling their auguring function as the poem's early harbingers of the Holocaust.

As mentioned above, such a foreshadowing mechanism consists of the dynamic nature of the textual sequence, in which late information that is unfolded along the textual continuum sheds a new, elucidating light on the information that is inlaid earlier along the textual continuum. Consequently, readers are compelled to practice a "reverse reading." They must return to the early information, updating (or even deleting) the way it was previously comprehended (either partially or wrongly). Then the dated, erroneous comprehension must be replaced with a new comprehension, one that stems from the new light cast on it by the later, more updated information.

Hence, all the poem's early hints to the Holocaust cannot be completely, persuasively, or validly connected to the Holocaust until the poem reaches its end. Here, late information unveils the poem's true nature as a Holocaust poem (by relating to the six million slaughtered Jews). Nevertheless, those hints earn their foreshadowing function since they proved sufficient information that guides, goads, and leads the reader to crack and decode their cryptic character, as well as their connection to the Holocaust. Thus, what is considered, in an early stage of the poem's unfolding textual continuum, as an opaque, possible connection to the Holocaust is found out to be an adamantine connection to it. This, when the poem's latest information unearths itself and casts an informative, confirming light on the poem's earlier information (the literary hints). The latter displays its aesthetic capacity in the most formidable fashion in the following demonstration of the reciprocal interaction between the early and the late bodies of information, which are planted along the textual continuum. In the beginning of the poem, one reads about "a blossoming tree," as well as about the "softness of the spring." Undoubtedly, the spring stands for light that dawns after the darkness of the winter. At the end of the poem, however, one encounters the Holocaust.

Hence, the above weaves a pattern that consists of the following three components: a blossoming tree, bountifully flowing light (the streaming, dawning light of the spring), and the most atrocious slaughter of Jews. All those three, while mutually interacting in one pattern, are indeed an intricately spun allusion to a line in a long, renowned poem by Chaim Nachman Bialik (1873-1934), who is considered the greatest poet in the history of modern Hebrew literature. The title of that poem is "*Be'ir haHaregah*" (In the City of Slaughter), which Bialik composed in 1905, after the horrendous pogrom in the Russian-ruled town of Kishinev, Bessarabia, in which many Jews—men, women, children, and babies—were murdered.

As in this poem by Amichai, Bialik's expressed a flaming wrath against God, who remained shamefully indifferent when His nation was slaughtered by beasts of prey. As in Amichai's poem in focus, Bialik's (or rather, his poem's narrator, guided by the poem's implied author) enlists three elements that mutually cooperate. This is similar to the pattern mentioned above (one that obviously acts in capacity of a complex allusion to Bialik's). Hence the following line from Bialik's fervently furious "*In the City of Slaughter*" reads: "The sun was shining, the tree [acacia tree] was blossoming, and the slaughterer was slaughtering." The third phrase operates in capacity of a shocking punch line. Hence, it forms a hideous, murderous peak after two consecutive peaceful, placid, serene lines (in term of content, as well as rhetoric). Most certainly, such a punch line produces a startling, astounding surprise. It is one that further reinforces both the pogroms' atrocities and God's unforgivable indifference as He observes, as if paralyzed, those atrocities from His lofty, elevated viewpoint.

The allusion to Bialik's verses is further made laudably intricate and aesthetically complex and rewarding by the fact that the allusion's three components (the blossoming tree, the spring's light, and the murderous atrocities) are not amalgamated as they are in Bialik's but instead are scattered and dispersed along the poem's textual sequence.

Correspondingly, in order to notice and trace the allusion to Bialik's poem in the verses here under analysis, readers are compelled to practice an intellectual and analytical process. They must track the pieces of the allusive puzzle and combine them in the way that echoes Bialik's poem, where the alluded mosaiclike components are put together. Accordingly, such an approach focuses on the work of art's aesthetic mechanism in order to decipher it, to crack its cryptic machinery, to unravel it.

This approach to a Holocaust poem, imbued with all of its intensely emotional elements, compels the work of art's surgeon/scientist to keep an emotional distance from it. The distance is crucial since an emotional involvement clouds, blurs, and eclipses the literary scientist's capacity to perform an objective analysis.

Hence, dispersing and scattering the three allusive elements in Amichai's poem (the spring's light, the blossoming tree, and the slaughter) in three separate places along the poem's textual sequence, the reader is compelled to conduct an intelligent, rational process of reconstructing and gluing the allusive mosaic pieces and discerning in this way their orchestrated, synchronic operation as one united allusion to Bialik's. By utilizing this process, overemotionality and sentimentality will be effectively bridled, tempered, and muted.

As it is beautifully put in Yehuda Amichai's poem *A Dangerous Love*:

All night long I was sitting awake, at home
In order to separate words from emotions,
Like a stamp collector who detaches stamps from the envelopes
In order to put them together in straight, colorful lines.

Indeed, Amichai's poem in focus displays aesthetic faculties at their most desirable zenith. However, above that elevated artistic vertex hovers the poem's scorching chastisement against God, who murmured to Himself "Buona Notte" before He retired to His comfortable chambers. And His "Arrivederci" was too feeble, too frail—never to be heard.

Portrait of an Airport as a Bloodthirsty Death Camp

The Poem "Little Ruth"

Little Ruth

Sometimes I recollect you, little Ruth.
We parted in our distant childhood,
they burnt you in the death camp.
Had you lived now, you would have been
a woman of sixty five years of age.
A woman on the threshold of old age.
You were burnt in the camp when
you were twenty years old.

And I don't know what happened to you
during your short life
Since we parted. What you accomplished, what ranks
Had decorated your shoulders, your sleeves,
Your fearless soul, what glowing, gleaming stars
They glued to your chest, what bravery medals, what
Medals of love they hung on your neck,
What peace upon you, may your memory be for peace.
And what happened to your unused years?
Are they still packed like pretty parcels,
Had they been added to my life? Had you made me
Your love bank, like the banks in Switzerland

In which the concealed treasure is kept
also after its owner's death?
Shall I bequeath all of that to my children
Whom you have never seen?

You bestowed your life upon me,
like a seller of intoxicating
Wine, but he stays sober,
Sober of death like yourself, lucid like
the satanic nether world
For a life drunk like myself, who rolls in
his forgetfulness.
Sometimes I remember you in times
That I have not anticipated and in sites
not made for remembrance,
But only for the passenger who never stays;
Like in the airport when the arriving passengers
Stand exhausted by the baggage carousel
That brings their suitcases and packages,
And they cry cheerfully upon tracking
down their luggage
Like experiencing resurrection
and they leave for their lives.

And there is one suitcase that keeps
returning and disappearing
And returning again, slowly,
in the empty luggage hall,
And again and again it is passing by,
Like your silent image that is passing by my face,

This way I remember you, until
The carousel quits circulating.
And does keep quiet. Selah.

"Little Ruth" was Yehuda Amichai's childhood friend in Germany. Later, when the Nazi spirit had started rocking Germany, peeling off its camouflage of bountiful culture while unveiling its venomous, underlying currents, Amichai's family fled from the forthcoming inferno and set down roots in the land of Israel. Ruth's family, however, still cultivated hope that the forceful tempest would eventually calm down, and its toxin would fade away and disappear like a bad dream. That hope, however, tragically proved to be morbid naivete. Hence, little Ruth found her dreadful death, executed by the Nazis.

The poem's overture shares with the reader, in a nutshell fashion, the comprehensive content of the poem, one that is about to be critically analyzed along the unfolded poem's textual continuum. In this respect, the poem may be metaphorically compared with a mosaic, or a puzzle, as the poem's numerous parts are already drawn in its few commencing lines.

The narrator's statement—"You were burnt in the camp when you were twenty years old"—is undoubtedly a piercingly chilling, hair-raising expression. Besides the latter, however, that expression allusively echoes a proverbial saying in the Talmudic volume *Pirkey Avot* (Lessons [of wisdom] of the Fathers [the Talmudic sages]). That proverbial saying attempts to portray and document the evolving stages in a man's life: "At five years of age, the study of the

Scriptures; At ten, the study of the Mishna; at fifteen, the study of the Talmud; At eighteen, marriage; At twenty, pursuit of livelihood; At thirty, the peak of strength; At forty, wisdom; At fifty, able to give counsel; at sixty, old age creeping on; At seventy, fullness of years; At ninety, the body bends; At one hundred, as good as dead, and gone completely out of the world."

Hence, the poem's statement regarding little, Ruth—"You were burnt in the camps when you were twenty years old"—produces an acidly ironical, and equally bitterly sarcastic, allusion to the Talmudic quote: "At twenty, pursuit of livelihood." Hence, instead of pursuing her livelihood at the age of twenty (according to the Talmudic saying), death pursued her.

That bitterly mordant irony serves simultaneously two literary functions of singular importance. First, such a piercingly caustic irony is aimed at God, who enabled such a massacre in which at twenty Ruth found her death instead of celebrating livelihood, according to the Talmudic saying. This literary function (that is conceived by the literary allusion to the Talmud's saying) consists of moral characteristics.

Hence, it expresses the poem's throbbingly outraged "*j'accuse*" against the murky, bleak world, one that is devoid of God, mercy, and justice. Thus, the acidly scalding irony is a literary device that is harnessed to the poem's moral credo and equally serves it. The other literary function, fulfilled by the blatantly bitter allusion to the Talmudic saying in focus, is of an aesthetic merit. Accordingly, irony consists of distance between two expressions, a surface one and a latent one. The distance, however, can be between two levels of awareness. In this case, however, the distance that is produced by the irony is between the reader and the text. Such a distance is both desirable and worthy since it blocks and dams a flood of emotions, which can be translated into vulgar sentimentality. Thus, the irony in focus serves well the poem's aesthetic texture by keeping it away from the lurking snare of outlandish, kitschy sentimentality.

As the reader further witnesses, the irony and its paramount contribution to the artistic value of the poem does not end at this early stage since it continues introducing itself and operating through the termination of the poem. The following text confirms the latter:

...what ranks
Had decorated your shoulders, your sleeves,
Your fearless soul, what glowing, gleaming stars
They glued to your chest, what bravery medals, what
Medals of love they hung on your neck...

The decorating medals and ranks, as well as the glowing, gleaming stars, both ironically and sarcastically allude to the yellow Jewish star (the star of David) that the tormented and humiliated Jews had been forced to wear on their chest during the Holocaust. Hence, the medals, ranks, and the stars—originally a source of pride—are ironically metamorphosed in the poem as they signify the Nazis' brutality.

The phrase "what/Medals of love they hung on your neck" turns the bitterly blatant irony into a mortal one as it alludes to the act of hanging. This is one of the ways which the Nazis used to murder their victims. The following phrase is no less blatantly and bitterly ironic: "What peace upon you, may your memory be for peace." The expression "peace upon you" is an allusion to a phrase from the Jewish prayer for the dead (*kaddish*, derives from the Hebrew word *kaddosh*, meaning "Holy"): "He Who spreads peace in His celestial heights, may confer peace upon us and upon all Israel, and let us say Amen."

The conclusion of the poem's phrase in focus—"may your memory be of peace"—alludes to a phrase recited upon the death of a person: "May his memory be for a blessing." This way, the mortal allusion in focus is reinforced by the second allusion to death. Hence, the seemingly innocent reference to peace upon Ruth is found to be a morbidly ironical allusion to death, to Ruth's terrible termination. The unbridgeable gulf between soothing peace and acid death endows the poem's critical irony with a further sense of furious fatality. The following bulk of text introduced in the poem marks a dramatically unexpected revolution. Accordingly, just as it is introduced, the narrator goes through a surprising metamorphosis. Although he continues to display much compassion to "little Ruth," the previously pure compassion is colored in the newly introduced bulk of text by opportunistic, egoist inclinations:

And what happened to your unused years?
Are they still packed like pretty parcels,
Had they been added to my life? Had you made me
Your love bank, like the banks of Switzerland

In which the concealed treasure is kept also after its owner's death?
Shall I bequeath all of that to my children
Whom you have never seen?

The narrator's question about dead Ruth's "unused years" causes the reader to raise a surprised eyebrow, while igniting his/her investigative curiosity. Accordingly, the narrator's choice of the words, "unused years," may bring to mind an expression like "used cars" (or a similar one that relates to used merchandise), commonly employed by used car dealers. Also dealers of scrap iron and junk, or sellers in a garage sale, can use a similar expression that contains the word used.

The narrator's wish that dead Ruth's "unused years" be added to his own life makes him look like a greedy, egoistically motivated person. Hence, the narrator who lamented little Ruth's brutal death is revealed as a voracious, grasping, shrewdly calculating person who desires to benefit from little Ruth's tragic death. His/Her own verbal formulation portrays him as a cynical opportunist, as a petty peddler who distastefully wishes to scavenge on the "unused years" left by a murdered childhood friend. The following bulk of text continues that inclination by portraying the narrator as a person of repellent eagerness who wishes to translate his/her friend's death into a merit on his part:

Had you made me
Your love bank, like the banks in Switzerland

In which the concealed treasure is kept also
after its owner's death?
Shall I bequeath all of that to my children ...

The reference to Swiss banks brings to mind a sharp businessman, dressed elegantly and carrying an expensive, leather briefcase. Nevertheless, the stylish businessman is no different from the insignificant peddler since both chase a "quick buck."

Hence, the narrator's previous portrayal, associated with touching compassion, is omitted and replaced by an eager narrator who aims to benefit from his/her childhood friend's death. The gap between the early narrator and the later one produces sarcastic irony that acts as a scalding reprimand against the narrator. Most certainly, such a dramatic and unexpected change in the narrator's portrayal conceives a rhetorical device of frustrated expectations. The new, unappealing narrator creates a gulf of identification between himself/herself and the reader. That gulf is equally a rational distance between the reader and the text, one that helps to push away any taint of undesirable sentimentality.

The following bulk of text continues the ironical inclination in focus:

You bestowed your life upon me, like a seller of
intoxicating
Wine, but he stays sober,
Sober of death like yourself, lucid like the satanic
nether world,

For a life drunk like myself, who rolls in his forgetfulness.

Again, the narrator is presented in a negative fashion while he continues benefiting from Ruth's death. Accordingly, her death is not a terminal one because her life is transferred to the narrator. However, her lost life, which is planted in the narrator's, makes him/her look like a drunk person "who rolls in his/her forgetfulness."

Although the criticism that aims at the narrator in this part of the poem is not as chastising as the previous one, the inclination to rebuke the narrator continues to maintain its momentum. The gulf between the early compassionate narrator and the later one continues being both surprising and ironical. As previously mentioned, since irony is based on a gulf between two entities (in this case the gulf between the two narrators), it does form a distance.

The poem concludes with the following two stanzas:

Sometimes I remember you in times
That I have not anticipated and in sites not made for remembrance,
But only for the passenger who never stays;
Like in the airport when the arriving passengers
Stand exhausted by the baggage carousel
And they cry cheerfully upon tracking down their luggage
Like experiencing resurrection and they leave for their lives.

And there is one suitcase that keeps
returning and disappearing
And returning again, slowly, in the empty
luggage hall,
And again and again it is passing by,
Like your silent image that is passing by my face,
This way I remember you, until
The carousel quits circulating.
And does keep quiet. Selah.

Like in the previous two stanzas, a surprise awaits the reader. In these two stanzas, the compassionate early narrator turns into an egoistic, greedy one. That change produced an ironical surprise. In the poem's last two stanzas, however, the early narrator is resurrected. He returns to his compassionate self while remembering little Ruth with pity and pining. The latter is metaphorically embodied by the single, lonely suitcase that remains on the airport's luggage carousel and nobody comes to claim it. The deserted suitcase is metaphorically associated with death, as if its owner died and will never pick it up.

Terminating the poem with the same compassionate early narrator (while portraying the narrator, in the middle of the poem, as a greedy and selfish person) produces a sense of circularity. It is as if the poem is wrapped from both polar sides by an appealing narrator, while in the middle the unappealing narrator is nesting. That circularity may be considered a compositional device that reinforces the unity of the poem. The shift from the early narrator to the middle one, and the reverse shift—at the poem's conclusion—back to the early narrator, operates as a swinging pendulum. Its oscillations confer a touch of energetic vitality on the poem's textual sequence.

The resurrection of the early narrator at the end of the poem may metaphorically be compared with the resurrection of little Ruth, in the thoughts and feelings of the narrator. In this respect, the poem displays a tinge of optimism, despite its gloom and doom content and atmosphere. Death is not as ultimate as we sometimes believe. We continue living in the memories of our loved ones.

A Train Trip to Satan's Territory

The Poem "My Son, My Son, My Head, My Head"

Absalom my son, my son Absalom; If only I
had died instead of you; Oh Absalom, my son, my son.
(2 Samuel 18:33)

My Son, My Son, My Head, My Head

My son, my son, my head, my head,
Riding this train I am going through
A foreign landscape, reading about Auschwitz
And learning the difference
Between "to leave" and "not to stay."

My son, my head, my son, my head.
The roads are wet like a drowned woman
Who was pulled out of the river as dawn broke
After a frantic search of delirious lights.
Now it is quiet:
A dead body beams.

My head, my head, my son, my son!
The lack of capability to define pain precisely
Makes it difficult for physicians to trace an illness
And forever deprives us of
Loving truly.

One of the most noticeable aesthetic-rhetorical phenomenon in this poem is the first line that commences each of the poem's three stanzas. It clearly reads—and indeed sounds—like an echoing lament, a tormented, mournful cry of a person hurt, haunted, and suffering over the loss of a son. This heartbreaking cry repeats (with slight changes that will be discussed later) three times; and each time, this mournful lament opens the stanza. This confers on the cry two qualities of pounding rhetoric.

The first is that the repetitions of the mourning, lamenting cry triples its rhetorical echo. Second, placing that mournful cry at the very beginning of each stanza further reinforces its rhetorical power. Therefore, the beginning (like the ending) of each and every text is the most powerful point when it comes to rhetorical potency and impact. While the thrice-iterated lament, placed in the most powerful rhetorical spot, is endowed with a uniquely echoing sound, the repetition may also create and introduce a poetic peril.

Accordingly, a too tight, precise repetition may produce an undesirable result—one of rigidity, automatization, mechanization, and a lifeless lack of flexibility. To combat this, each of the three cries exhibits compositional changes (that consist of the order in which the words are placed in the syntactical unit), which injects a desirable lively rhetorical flexibility into the repetition pattern. In this way, the poem will cultivate a prudent, aesthetically meritorious balance between rhetorical pounding reflections, on the one hand, and appealing rhetorical animated flexibility, on the other.

The thematic nature of that lamenting cry, one that keeps repeating "my head, my head," yields a piercing impression of a man who is holding his bent down head with his hands, while forcefully pressing his pounding temples, as if to silence the shriek that is causing his head to throb (reminiscent of a powerful Van Gogh painting). Most certainly, that visual reflection of the verbal cry further reinforces the latter's forceful vocal vibrations, its puissant presence. Undoubtedly, the fact that the echoing, haunting lament is based on a biblical allusion considerably enhances its steel-like forcefulness.

That Biblical allusion takes the reader to King David, lamenting and mourning the death of his beloved son Absalom, who was killed during the rebellion that he led against his own father. This betrayal neither eclipses nor clouds King David's fervent love for his rebellious son. Correspondingly, that fact does not block or mute David's bitter lament, which follows his son's death: "Oh my son, Absalom my son, my son Absalom; If only I had died instead of you; Oh Absalom my son my son" (2 Samuel 18). And later: 'The King hid his face and cried aloud, "My son Absalom, oh, Absalom, my son, my son" (ibid., 19:4).

Like the person in the poem echoing a heartrending cry, King David cannot stop repeating the same two words in his mourning lament. Further, David's gesture of grief, in which he hides his face and thus holds his head with his hands, is also echoed meticulously in the poem (as alluded to by "my head, my head"). One may also trace here a visual allusion to the famous expressionist painting *The Cry* by the Norwegian artist Edvard Munch.

From the above, one can tell, and equally appreciate, how cleverly and effectively the poem sculpts and activates that piercing cry of chastising mourning and haunting lament. This cry translates into a shocking scream, into a thundering shriek, in reaction to the Holocaust.

Nevertheless, the poem proves persuasively that it knows how to cultivate feelings, while avoiding the snare of excessive emotion and sentiment. For that prudently practiced aesthetic performance, the poem creates an alienating distance between the narrator and the text (which alludes to the Holocaust) and, correspondingly, between the reader and the text. That distance is extremely important in an effort to address an immensely charged topic, while avoiding the lurking trap of vulgar, kitschy sentimentality. Accordingly, only an alienating distance can block an emotional identification with the topic in focus; and only a lack of this identification with the topic portrayed in the poem (of this art category) avoids over-emotionality and arrests sentimentality. The latter turn toward distance is especially crucial when the topic is the Holocaust, the arch-quarry of emotions. All the above is successfully exercised throughout the poem's entire textual sequence.

My son, my son, my head, my head,
Riding this train I am going through
A foreign landscape, reading about Auschwitz
And learning the difference
Between "to leave" and "not to stay."

The viewpoint of the poem's narrator is exhibited while he is riding a train, probably in Germany (or somewhere else in Europe) as one can conclude from "going through/ A foreign landscape." A huge gap is yawned between the piercingly mournful and haunting lament that opens the stanza ("My son, my son, my head, my head") and the rest of the stanza, in which he displays perfect peace and cold tranquility (while riding the train he is reading and educating himself). This rift—which can be depicted as an abyss—is essential in further battling sentimentality. It yields a rhetorical distance, one that is dexterously translated into a barrier that dams and blocks emotional identification and, correspondingly, prevents the peril of too much sentiment.

The above is also evident when relating to the train in the poem's opening stanza. Initially, it brings to mind trains that heartlessly transferred millions of Jews—including one million children and infants—to the Nazi death camps and gas chambers. Yet, the narrator is sitting comfortably, peacefully in that train—reading, learning, watching the view—while acting like a pleased tourist who indulges himself/herself with an enjoyable vacation.

Hence, the reference to the train produces two dramatically different quarries of connotations that are drastically separated by the gap mentioned previously. As before, this produces a distance that prevents the possibility that emotionality shall be evoked by the text. In this way, the poem once again avoids the risk of being snared by sentimentality, where an excess of emotions would prevail, causing feelings to become vulgar and tasteless. The fact that the narrator is "going through/A foreign landscape," further reinforces the employed aesthetic policy of producing estrangement, alienation, gap, distance, which all act in capacity of an effective precaution against emotional identification and sentimentality.

Such is also the case in which the narrator is "reading about Auschwitz/And learning...." There is an immense chasm between the scorching emotions evoked by the atrocities committed in Auschwitz and the narrator's scientific, scholarly, cold-minded reading about Auschwitz, devoid of even a sliver of emotion. This gap also translates into a distance that drastically curbs and restrains feelings while simultaneously effectively suffocating even a faint hint of sentiment.

The concluding statement of this stanza seems rather puzzling: "the difference/Between 'to leave' and 'not to stay.'" What is the reason, the need, for tracing the subtle semantic-linguistic difference between those two terms that basically mean the same thing? And on what grounds is that semantic-linguistic inquiry engaged with the poem? Apparently, and upon considering the poem's topic, which is the Holocaust, those two terms are associated with Jews who left Europe prior to the Shoah.

There is a difference (which translates into a distance, the poem's most effective way to dim emotions and arrest sentimentality) between leaving and not staying. To *leave* means to be active and initiate a departure. *Not to stay* means to leave passively because there is no other route to take. However, on a metaphorical level, both to *leave* and *not to stay* may mean leaving—either actively or passively—the land of the living. Most certainly, the poem's Holocaust context bestows persuasive validity upon that metaphorical interpretation. Correspondingly, a blatantly bitter irony is traced in the difference between the active leaving (to leave) and the passive leaving (not to stay), once they are comprehended metaphorically. Accordingly, this difference that may be significant (on moral, psychological grounds, for instance) under normal circumstances had been ironically and horribly erased and faded away under the Nazi's circumstances. Thus all leavers—the active ones and the passive ones—together left the land of the living, while sharing the same degree of torment.

Irony, essentially, is founded upon a distance between two levels of awareness. Hence, the ironical distance hereby detected continues the poem's leading trend: to address the Holocaust, the most emotional-laden topic of all, while restraining emotionality and cleverly deviating from the aesthetically perilous track that leads to undesirable, tasteless sentimentality.

Being equipped with the insight introduced above, the reader further follows the poem's textual continuum and encounters the poem's second stanza:

My son, my head, my son, my head.
The roads are wet like a drowned woman
Who was pulled out of the river as dawn broke
After a frantic search of delirious lights.
Now it is quiet:
A dead body beams.

In regard to theme and topic, this second stanza is dramatically different from the first one, to the point that they do not seem to be part of the same poem. Such is also the case of the poem's third stanza: it seems to be entirely alien to both preceding stanzas. Hence, on a level of topic and theme, of chronicle and plot (as much plot as one may trace and detect in a lyrical poem), the poem's three stanzas surrender and deliver the impression that they are randomly amalgamated, glued to each other arbitrarily. However, only a systematic, rational, intellectually oriented process of interpretative analysis possesses the capacity to unearth the latent, cryptic common denominator that causally connects the three stanzas to each other. This constructs them as one poem displaying tight unity.

The preceding serves splendidly to dim and overcome excessive emotionality and to nip even the tiniest bud of sentimentality—the enemy of worthy aesthetics. Accordingly, by rationally cracking and intellectually deciphering the cryptic code of the poem's unity, any reaction to its emotionally and sentimentally saturated content can be curbed effectively. A rational attitude leading to intellectual activity can only materialize when the literary text is probed from a scientific distance. This is analogous to a surgeon who is performing an operation with cold professionalism. Also, analyzing the literary text in this manner may be metaphorically compared to a laboratory test that in order to be successful cannot afford cultivating an emotional attitude. Thus, the poem is sculpted in such a way that the reader is compelled to peel its epidermic layer —that seems to be devoid of feeling—which will unearth its latent logical structure. This guarantees success in the aesthetically crucial battle against undesirable elements contained within.

Continuing the interpretative process (initiated with the scientific analysis of the poem's first stanza), it may be convenient for the reader to have the second stanza repeated.

My son, my head, my son, my head.
The roads are wet like a drowned woman
Who was pulled out of the river as dawn broke
After a frantic search of delirious lights.
Now it is quiet:
A dead body beams.

The first line, which repeats the narrator's mournful cry—while echoing King David's lament upon the death of Absalom, his son—was already discussed in detail. Nevertheless, it is paramount to stress the importance of the automatic repetition in the biblical lament, as it is so plausibly displayed in David's lamentation. It basically consists of two words only—*Absalom, my son* (the latter in Hebrew is one word only, *b'ni*)—that keeps repeating and repeating, like a pounding hammer. Hence, the fact that the grief-filled line, which opens the poem's first stanza, reappears at the commencement of the poem's second stanza, and yields further repetition (beyond the verbal repetition that is *in esse* in the lament itself) on both the level of verbality (the same words keep repeating) and composition (both lamenting cries are placed in the two stanza's first line).

Since repetition is the very essence of the biblical lament (echoed in the poem), further fortifying that principal repetition with one more (which consists of two separate repetitions: compositional and verbal), reinforces the poem's lament and makes its echo dramatically louder.

In the poem's first stanza, the reference to a train operates as a metonym for the Nazi trains that transferred the Jews in atrociously inhumane conditions to their death. A similar metonym is traced in the poem's second stanza as well. In this case, however, it is not as direct and clear as in the first stanza, although it is equally as persuasive and valid.

That second metonym is the wet roads found in the second stanza. Like the trains, the roads also served the Nazis to transfer Jews (just as other deadly devices were used to slaughter Jews) from most of the European countries, mainly to Poland, where the Nazis built the death camps. Portraying the roads as being wet may metaphorically reflect the later attempt by most Germans to wipe off their mark of Cain: as the rain washes away the road's dust, stains, and soil, so the Nazis and too many of their offspring have tried to wash away, from both their conscience and history, the murderous stains, squalor, and shame.

Most certainly, the repetition of two metonyms, for the Nazi's deadly means of transporting Jews to the gas chambers, further emphasizes the somber sound of a lament in the poem. This is due to the lament's nature (following the biblical model) that is founded upon echoing repetitions. Also, the echoing of two metonyms for the Nazis' murderous transportation is countered by a semantic difference between the two in focus: a train in the first stanza, wet roads in the second. That difference carries aesthetic merit: it inserts a change into the mechanically repeating lament unit, and, consequently, it injects flexibility to the repeating pattern. This keeps it from turning into a stiff, rigid automatism, without eclipsing the lament's repetition characteristics.

The major image in the poem's second stanza consists of the following simile:

The roads are wet like a drowned woman
Who was pulled out of the river as dawn broke
After a frantic search of delirious lights.

The drowned woman brings to mind David's son, Absalom, who was famous for his long, beautiful, womanlike hair. Absalom's death stemmed from his long hair getting caught and entangled in the ramified branches of an oak tree, which suffocated him (the feminine connotations are fortified here since the oak tree mentioned in Absalom's death is feminine: *elah*, unlike the more common use in masculine: *alon*).

Hence, focusing on a metaphorically portrayed dead woman in the poem's second stanza bring to mind biblical Absalom (whose hair was like a woman's). King David' lament, after his son's death, acts as a model for the lament that is molded in this poem. In light of the above, alluding to Absalom's death through the metaphorical portrayal of the drowned woman in the second stanza is one more way that David's powerful, moving words are echoed. Naturally, this biblical reference not only enhances the poem's aesthetic intricacy (displayed by the appealing and complex characteristics of that allusion), but also further reinforces the poem's touching lament and somber, sad sound of mourning.

Most certainly, the metaphorical image of a nocturnal, frantic search with delirious lights, that ends with absolute silence—in which the dead body of the drowned woman lies beaming in the bright, sterilized, acid, cold, deadly light of the morgue—creates the most earsplitting contrast. The frenzied nocturnal havoc that ends, as dawn breaks—with mortal tranquility and still, soundless death —imparts the most clashing impact, one that violently, even wildly, makes the reader shudder, shiver, and quiver.

On the poem's verbal surface, that startling shift of events confers on the text a dramatic quality, which may be metaphorically portrayed as a bomb blast. The latter, most certainly, is in cogent congruence with the poem's shocking topic, the Holocaust. Thus, the jarring rapid change—from the frantic nocturnal scene to the mortal, silent one—may justly be considered a prudently formed metaphor that reflects and portrays the Holocaust's barbaric character.

This explosive shift further metaphorically reflects the Holocaust: After the violent havoc of the mass murder, deadly silence had settled. Hence the two portions of the metaphorically molded image that controls the second stanza (the violent frenzy that abruptly metamorphized into mortal, lethal silence); and the reciprocal interaction between the two reflect the Holocaust twice, from two different and equally complementary perspectives.

Most certainly, the above not only enhances the poem's aesthetic complexity, but it also does a valuable service for the poem's angry message: engrave the Holocaust on your heart, never let it be evicted from your memory. Still further. The metaphorical image of the drowned woman may testify differently about the Holocaust. Indeed, the hectic search for her body, during the entire night, justly evokes the impression of modern times, in which all technological means, powerful spotlights and laudable human efforts are invested in a search for a lost person in a stormy river.

Nevertheless, the poem is far from implying such times. Instead, it suggests a period when God gave in and the devil took over, and prevailed. In this respect, the humanistic, praiseworthy search for a drowned (or lost) person, in the dead of night; the determined urge to find her even if she is dead, in order to bring her to an honorable burial—such a noble human quality is exceedingly alien to the period of time portrayed in the poem. Thus, in order to comprehend the metaphorical role of the drowned woman, one has to peel away the background chronicle that narrates the nocturnal search for her, while poetically probing only her fictional character. Only when the drowned woman is isolated from the background story of that search (since that humanistic story is not feasible in the context of the Holocaust) and is examined following extrication from that misleading context is one in a position to consider what follows.

The drowned woman in the river echoes her countless sisters during the dark, bleak, sinister medieval period in Europe. This includes Germany, the master architect and executor of the Holocaust. For a variety of evil and mendacious reasons, those women were accused of practicing witchcraft. They were trapped in that wicked plot, in that snaring conspiracy, while being doomed to their deadly end. Hence, in all those cases, the local prince set the following test. The wrongly accused woman is thrown into the river's tempestuous water, with a heavy stone tightly knotted to her neck.

If she floats, despite the rock that is pulling her down to the river's deadly floor, it means that she is innocent. If she drowns, however, it shall be a cogent sign that she is guilty. One can imagine, of course, how many women did indeed float with this heavy load tied to their necks. Hence, in this way, countless innocent women were cruelly executed through agonizing drowning, due to their rulers' evil character, one devoid of even a hint of mercy. Such a metaphorical understanding of the drowned woman in the poem's second stanza casts an elucidating light on her and enables the reader to follow insightfully her symbolic role in a poem that focuses on the Holocaust.

Upon superficially studying the poem's textual surface, one may justly introduce the question: What is the connection between that drowned woman and the Holocaust? In which capacity does she appear and act in the poem? However, only when the modern context of attempting to rescue or find the drowned woman is dismissed (due to its lack of relevance during the Holocaust) does the reader possess the capacity to decipher her metaphorical role in the poem. Accordingly, upon metaphorically alluding to countless innocent women, cruelly executed by sinister people in power during the bleak and murky Middle Ages, the drowned woman who died in great agony echoes countless innocent women (men and children as well) who were executed by the Nazis. This is one more plausible example that attests to the erroneous nature of the seemingly cogent adage: What you see is what you get. Regarding the drowned woman in the poem (one of a few examples), what you see is far from what you can and should get. Hence, on the poem's textual surface, the role she plays seems quite questionable, even perplexing. Yet, once the reader excavates and unveils the metaphorical genealogy of that drowned woman, then he/she is able to comprehend the woman's prominent role in the poem.

That insight leads us to the third and last stanza of the poem.

My head, my head, my son, my son!
The lack of capability to define pain precisely
Makes it difficult for physicians to trace an illness
And forever deprives us of
Loving truly.

Here is a wisely sculpted paradox: what stands out in this stanza is what is missing in it, in comparison with the two previous stanzas. That left out component that captures the reader's attention is the lack of a reference to the Nazi's means of transportation—a train in the first stanza, roads in the second. Utilizing those means of transportation, the Nazis would transfer their helpless, hopeless, and tormented victims to their terminal destination. The lack of a similar reference to this in the third and concluding stanza symbolically signals that no means of transportation is required anymore on the Nazi's part. Their mission, to transfer all the Jews (and other millions of innocent people such as communists, socialists, intellectuals who condemned the Nazi regime, brave people who hid Jews and were caught, gypsies, homosexuals, the mentally ill, and others) to the death camps, had been completed.

Therefore, no vehicles of transportation were required anymore. Indeed, one may challenge such an argument on a historical basis. However, a poem is a work of art that may use historical facts, but it is never committed to abide by their precise validity. It utilizes them for aesthetic, fictional purposes that are neither supposed nor expected to mirror the accuracy of historical facts. Because the poem's last stanza breaches and denies the pattern that was cultivated, preserved, and developed in the previous two stanzas, it operates in the capacity of a compositional-rhetorical deice. Like a bait or a signpost, it draws the reader's attention. This enables the reader to solve the riddle of that lack and, correspondingly, trace and comprehend its symbolic status.

Hence, the breach of the poem's internally nurtured pattern, consisting of the two consecutive references to the Nazis murderous means of transportation (a train, roads), confers upon the deficiency in the poem's last stanza a symbolic role that signals to the reader: since the Nazis completed their mission, no means of transportation is required any more. Thus, it is a compositional-rhetorical symbol acting as a harbinger of the deadly tiding: no means of transportation is needed anymore since all the tortured, plagued passengers had been delivered to the death camps and were exterminated there.

The third stanza's leading statement is the following:

The lack of capability to define pain precisely
Makes it difficult for physicians to trace an illness
And forever deprives us of
Loving truly.

Indeed, pain is not a tangible object that can be defined with scientific precision. Nevertheless, the latter should not erect a stumbling block that will either dim or dam the physician's capacity "to trace an illness." After all, countless physicians all over the world, on a daily basis, treat innumerable patients, whose pain is neither measurable nor can be defined with scientific accuracy. Still, the physicians successfully treat and cure many of those patients.

Thus, the statement mentioned above seems not only questionable, but equally devoid of empirical validity. Yet that evident lack of validity, identifying the very essence of the statement, operates in the capacity of a rhetorical signpost, one that lures and traps the reader's attention. Once the readers' attention is hooked and averted by this trap, they are in a promising position to crack the code, decipher the statement's enigmatic grounds, and, correspondingly, unearth the latent logic that is concealed under the surface.

The lack of both logic (one that is successfully tested countless times on a daily basis) and factual validity in that statement (regarding the definition of human pain), on the one hand, and relation to the immeasurable human pain in the context of the Holocaust, on the other, conveys an immensely tormenting, haunting agony, regarding human suffering in the Holocaust. Hence, the pain experienced, mostly by Jews (but by millions of other innocent people as well), is indeed beyond earthly measurement, beyond any human definition or comprehension. Such a horribly chasing, piercing pain must shock even the most experienced physician to the point of feeling helpless and hopeless in his ability to cure.

Thus, the poem's third stanza both deliberately and prudently displays in its showcase a factually invalid statement. This is done in order to attract and kindle readers' attention. It does this while encouraging and urging them to excavate in the poem's textual soil, to remove the surface factual invalidity, and unveil the internal, latent symbolic validity. This validity addresses human pain in the Holocaust, while enlisting a paradox and an oxymoron: it attempts to define and portray this pain only to prove and deliver the somber conclusion that human pain, in the Holocaust, is beyond earthly definition, measurement, estimate.

The poem ends with the following statement:

The lack of capability to define pain precisely
Forever deprives us of
Loving truly.

Here, again, it seems that the poem introduces one more statement that is devoid of factual, experimental, realistic validity. Accordingly, it appears rather logical that people who suffered to a point that is beyond words would be eager to love truly, in order to partially compensate for the dreadful suffering that they experienced during the Holocaust. As previously employed, a deliberately misleading statement is nothing but a rhetorical signpost that signals to the reader, that under the upper illogical, invalid statement, one may detect a cryptic, symbolic, valid and logical one.

Hence, the Holocaust's haunting, hounding inhuman pain had scarred its victims. It did this so gravely, so severely, to the point that it sterilized their emotional faculties, had made them emotional invalids, everlastingly incapable of feeling love to its fullest. This is the gloomy message that the poem surrenders. Like the previously traced one, it is a message that rhetorically attracts the reader by its factual invalidity, while the latter goads the reader to trace its cryptic, symbolic truth in the underlying currents of the text.

The fact that such a brief stanza, sculpts, orchestrates, and performs with twin devices (consisting of the tense gap between surface, factual invalidity, and cryptic symbolic validity)—and that in both cases the same aesthetic mechanism is dexterously harnessed to a global message—confers on this slim slice of text the most appealing poetic complexity. It is neither random nor arbitrary that the poem ends with the narrator's bitter lament that the Holocaust's haunting atrocities had not only tormented the victims to a point that is beyond human comprehension, but also had sterilized them emotionally, rendering them emotional cripples, devoid of the capacity to love truly, to the fullest. The Nazis had erased their victims' past; had made their present a land where the devil reigned; had suffocated their future in the gas chambers, or by burying them alive.

However, beyond the above, the Nazis, after failing to butcher the few survivors, robbed them of the last single thing that was left: the capacity to attain a modicum of soothing comfort by experiencing love to its fullest. Hence, this slim poem seems to introduce aesthetic dexterity and a humanistic lesson at their vertex. Aesthetically, it displays modest verbality, on the verge of oversimplicity, in its complex pile of poetic layers. Every layer is concealed by another layer, and all of them enlist aesthetic devices that deliberately introduce intricate perplexities or lack of logic. Those devices ignite readers' curiosity and goad them to trace the latent logic, the symbolic sense, under the upper, epidermic lack of logic.

That poetic complexity, however, neither eclipses nor clouds the poem's message of wrathful, yet merciful humanism. The Nazis inflicted such agony and gloom on their tortured victims, but failed to extinguish their ability to express and verbalize pain. Even though expressing this pain does not heal the wound, verbalizing it is like a soft breeze conferring on the sufferer some soothing, albeit temporary, relief.

Fervent Love Forever: Love Poems

A Love Poem

It started like that; it suddenly felt in the heart
Faint, feeble, light and happy, like
The way a person feels when his shoelace unties
And he bends down

Later came other days.

Now I feel like a Trojan horse
Of terrible loves,
Every night they break out and act franticly
But at dawn they return to the dark belly.

The first stanza introduces the most surprising, astonishing simile; the feeling in the heart that one experiences upon being in love, feeling of lightness, of happiness, is like the way a person feels when his shoelace unties and he bends down. However, the speaker does not say why that person bends down (obviously, to tighten his untied shoelace) and he places the words "And he bends down" in a separate line. This way the words "he bends down" earn considerable attention. Since the verb "to bend down" yields negative connotations (submissiveness, capitulation, surrender, submission, humiliation), placing it in a separate line stresses those negative connotations which act in the capacity of a foreshadowing hint that heralds the negative, undesirable nature of the love that will be introduced in a more advanced stage of the unfolding text.

The following, consecutive line, further reinforces the foreshadowing, negative nature of the verb "to bed down": "Later came other days." Since the first, previous days (of love, as indicated by the poem's title) were days of happiness, of feeling lightness, the words "other days" introduce opposite, undesirable connotations. In the poem's third, last stanza, the speaker metaphorically portrays himself as a Trojan horse.

In Homer's *Illiad,* the Trojan horse in which Odysseus and his warriors hid prior to launching their attack, is engaged with blatantly brutal connotations. Such connotations of murderous destruction are in congruence with the way the speaker depicts himself as a Trojan horse in whose body "terrible loves" "break out" franticly and "act frenziedly." However, in contrast to the Trojan horse which was engaged only one time with terror and havoc, the speaker as a Trojan horse is engaged with terrible, frantic, terrorizing loves night after night after night. Hence the peaceful, serene love in the poem's commencement, love that is even associated with connotations of humble, meek, submission, is metamorphosized in the poem's contusion and turns into a frantic, violent, destructive love.

Talking About Changes Was Talking Love

For a long time now I have not heard from you
I have not received from you even a piece of paper,
Even like one sent from formal offices
Which have already forgotten my name and
my very existence.

The generation machine is still sweet
Between my legs, but for a long time
now I have not felt
Between my eyes a sweetness of a letter.

We did not spend enough time together
For making us a monument of lovers.

Now time replaces time,
Sadness changes its people like people change clothes
And your serious face slices your life;
Every slice with another man.

And once we talked about changes
And talking about changes was talking love.

The first stanza testifies separation. That separation is introduced by the poem's speaker, who is agonized by frustrated, rejected love, broken love that has shattered his heart: he has not received from his rejecting lover even a note like a note sent by bureaucratic offices which have already forsaken his name and even his very existence.

The second stanza continues depicting his blatantly bitter lament while focusing on the following two: the echoing recollection of the past that was saturated with the sweetness of soothing love and the thorny bitterness of the present, one that is hopelessly devoid of love. The sweetness of the "generation machine" between his legs is an evocative, expressive metaphor for the sweet love making that he experienced in his unforgettable past; but at the very same tormenting, haunting time, he is deprived in the oppressive present of the sweetness of a letter from his denying beloved.

Indeed, not only the present but also the past is a subject of his mourning confession: he and his beloved did not spend enough time together for erecting a monument dedicated to their love. The reference to a monument is neither random nor arbitrary: it symbolizes the death of love, love that will never be resurrected.

> *"now time replaces time*
> *Sadness changes its people like people*
> *change clothes"*

Time may replace time. The present may replace the past but sadness is always sadness. Only the people who experience sadness change. Hence, even the glorious past, the past that was saturated with fervent love, was not devoid of a touch of sadness. That touch of sadness derived from the painfully short duration that was allocated for the lovers' togetherness. And that touch of sadness is the one that conceives and yields the morbid, deadly image of a monument, the one that metaphorically illustrates the death of love.

> *"And your serious face slices your life;*
> *Every slice with another man."*

The denied lover, the hurt one, portrays his rejecting beloved as a woman who is devoid of feelings, devoid of compassion, a woman who radiates arctic cold, a woman who treats her own life like a scientist in a lab, like a pathologist who slices a dead body. That and more. The rejected lover is also "plagued" by scalding, mordant jealousy: he portrays his rejecting beloved "distributing her life's slices to different men who step on the threshold of her life.

> *"And once we talked about changes*
> *And talking about changes was talking love."*

Talking about changes is talking love because when lovers talk about changes they talk about the future, the future of their togetherness. But now the rejecting beloved is gone. And her love is gone. And only the rejected lover is left, left alone, contaminated by the emptiness of the present, snared in frustration, besieged by both consuming pining and piercing pain.

An Old Stone House of Tools

What is it? It is an old stone house of tools.
No, it is great love that is gone.
Anxiety and happiness were in this darkness
And hope. Perhaps once I already was here
But I didn't get closer to see.

These cries emerge from a dream
No, this is great love
No, this is an old stone house of tools.

The speaker is facing a building that seems to him like an old stone house of tools. However, he immediately updates his initial observation by saying to himself:

"No, it is great love that is gone."

Hence, the flame of the fervent love of the past has been shamefully converted to a shabby, dated, poor-looking old stone-house of tools. The poem continues as following:

"Anxiety and happiness were in this darkness
And hope."

Hence, past and present are intertwined while darkness belongs to the tattered, a disheartening present, the past is presented by the traditional "harbingers" of "flammable" love: anxiety, happiness, hope. All of them are the well known "ingredients" of love in which pain and passion, fear, frustration and hope are reciprocally amalgamated. Indeed, the lover of the past, does not fail to recognize that place that once hosted fervent love. He does not fail to discern and unearth the love that has turned into disappointing, scalding ashes. Yet, he is devoid of the courage to face the scorching reality, reality in which the passionate, frenzied love has extinguished, has faded away, has been converted into ruins and ashes. Hence, instead of confronting the thorny reality, he is pretending that this place, the place of his past love, is *terra incognita* for him:

> *"Perhaps once I already was here*
> *But I didn't get closer to see."*

Indeed, he is leading himself astray: of course he got closer to see. That was his very love, after all. But reality is stronger than him. He keeps denying. And his denial is translated to another escape from agonizing reality: to a fictional reality of a dream: "These cries emerge from a dream." They don't. The dream is nothing but a wishful thinking, one that will never meet materialization. Yet, he still tries to kindle the aching memory of the extinguished love:

> *"No, this is great love"*

His desire to revive the love that faded, that died out, is so overpowering to the point that he starts speaking about the past love in preset tense ("is" instead of "was"). However, reality is stronger than his wishful thinking, his dream, his idle desire to find refuge in the past. Hence, he is compelled to confront reality, as bristly as it may be:

> *"No, this an old stonehouse of tools."*

This way, the speaker, the hurt lover, oscillates between the present and the past, between thorny reality and soothing dream, between what he wants and what he gets. And like his love in the past, he is withered, he is wilted, he is doomed to his haunting, tormenting uprootedness. He can neither resurrect the past, nor can he beautify the present. The past is beyond his reach, the present is not his shielding shelter. He is exiled from peace of mind, he is sentenced to shadowing frustration. He is uprooted. He has neither past nor present.

This Evening

This evening, I think again
About many days, which sacrificed themselves
For one night of love.
About the waste and about the fruit of the waste,
About the plenty and about the fire.
And how, with no pain, time.

I saw roads lead
From another man to another woman
I saw life erased
Like a letter in the rain.
I saw a table on which was placed

A bottle of wine and on its label was written "The Brothers"
And how, with no pain, time.

The concept "sacrifice" is associated with highly laudable connotations of desirable willingness to give up personal interests for the sake of a noble purpose. Therefore, stating that many days sacrificed themselves for the sake of one night of love puts that one night of love on the most elevated pedestal. However, the next consecutive line negates blatantly the highly elevated nature of that one night of love: "About the waste and about the fruit of that waste". Hence, that laudable sacrifice for the sake of one night of love was entirely worthless, gravely devoid of substance. That and more. That waste was even more sadly grievous since it conceived and yielded "the fruit of the waste." The following line, however, introduces a pressing question mark:

"About the plenty and about the fire"

What plenty? And what fire? These are the plenty and the fire of that plentiful, fervent, burning love. But we already know: that kindled, flame-like love failed to meet all cultivated expectations it was a waste that yielded waste. Such a blatantly bitter disappointment leads the speaker to utter the following philosophically oriented conclusion, one of the most subdued acceptance: "And how, with no pain, time". Hence, passing time erases everything: days, sacrifice, night of love, waste, the fruit of waste, plenty, fire, time erases even pain. The pain of separation. Nothing is left. Nothing survives. As the Latin adage puts it: "*tempus edax rerum*" Time devours everything. Indeed, it seems that also Kohelet (Ecclesiastes) echoes in the poem's lines of docile submission:

> *"Utter futility, said Kohelet, utter futility"*
> *(Ecclesiastes 1:2)*

At the end of the day, at the end of all days, everything loses substance, everything is devoid of meaning, everything is nothing but dust and ashes. In the following, next stanza of the poem, the speaker presents the following confession:

> *"I saw roads lead*
> *From another man to another woman."*

On the one hand, these two lines may be considered positive as they attest to a reciprocal interaction between a man and a woman, very likely lovers. On the other hand, depicting them as "another man" and "another woman" does yield and radiate a sense of alienation, of remoteness, of strangeness. One may put it in the following fashion: once that man and that woman are "another man", "another woman", a chill wall of foreigness separates them.

And what about life? What about the essence of life? Life is as erased as a letter in the rain. A letter, a symbol of communication, of a reciprocal interaction, of closeness, is erased by the rain. A manifestation of total elimination, of total termination. And life is as erased as a letter erased by the rain.

And what about the table? Nobody sits by the table. Neither a man nor a woman. Nobody. The table is as lifeless as a letter erased by the rain. As life is erased, as life is left lifeless. The only thing that is left, the only thing that survived (for the time being) is a bottle of wine. The speaker, however, does not miss the opportunity to conceive and yield a touch of bitter irony, perhaps even sardonic sarcasm. The label on the bottle of wine says "The Brothers."

The connotations of brotherhood are closeness, unity, solidarity. Everything that all the poem's components lack. Everything that the "another man" and the "another woman" lack. The one night of love is a waste. A waste that conceives a waste. The plenty and the fire lead to nowhere. Indeed, they extinguished a long time ago. Life is erased like a letter in the rain. The table is deserted. And the label on the deserted bottle of line sarcastically stresses the barrenness shared by all the poem's components.

What is left? Nothing is left. No wonder the poem ends with the very same words with which it concluded the first stanza: "And how, with no pain, time." The barrenness, the lifelessness, the nothingness are so profoundly rooted, that even pain is not left. What is left? Nothing is left.

"Utter vanity...Utter vanity."
"Tempus edax rerum."

Our Love Has Reached Its Termination

Our love has reached its termination.
The time's defense walls are breached,
The brave deceitfulnesses collapse one by one.

My city, Jerusalem, is a stage
On which I perform from time to time
In a tragic gesture.
Jerusalem remembers similar gestures performed by
*Jeremiah with his "my bowls, my bowls"**
Frantic bag-pipes,
A sensitive mine of weeping and wailing.

Our love has reached its termination.
Pretty soon
The old, dull knives
Wil be ready for a new battle of pain and spectacle.

*Jeremiah 4:19

Also this love poem, like many love poems by Yehuda Amichai, laments the painful collapse of love, love that has withered, has wilted in the past while eclipsing the present and robbing the future of even a sliver of hope. In the first stanza, the downfall of love is portrayed in terms adopted from a defeat in war: "defense walls are breached"; "brave." The breached defense walls bring to mind wars in ancient times (such as Biblical times) when garrisons and fortified cities were protected by massive walls that eventually had been crushed after being attacked and pounded by the enemy that besieged them.

Time is expected to protect the present from the grievous offences of the past. Not in this love poem, however. In this love poem, time is portrayed like defense walls which fail to defend. Those defense walls are shattered, are wrecked, are knocked down.

"*Tempus edax rerum*"? "Time devours everything"? Not in this poem of painfully extinguished love. And which are the "brave deceitfulnesses"? Those are the false, idle attempts to silence the scorching truth about the fading of the previously fervent love.

The city of Jerusalem is depicted as a stage in a theater on which the disappointed, frustrated, hurt speaker performs from time to time. He entitles his performance "a tragic gesture" ("tragic gesture" instead of "tragic play" like in Greek tragedy). In the original Hebrew text, there is a pun (which is lost in the English translation: he performs *mechvah* (a gesture) instead of *machazeh* (a play). This pun is neither random nor arbitrary. The past fervently tempestuous love which has become a faint, faded, diminished memory, is metaphorically reflected by the transformation of the majesty, splendor of a tragedy into a superficiality of a gesture. Yet, the speaker is haunted, tormented by the scalding, feverish memories of the flames of love which he experienced in the distant, misty past. Since he cannot defend himself from the flowing eruption of those raging memories, he transfers them to the city of Jerusalem:

> *"Jerusalem remembers similar gestures performed by Jeremiah with his "my bowls, my bowls"*

Frantic bagpipes,
A sensitive mine of weeping and wailing".

Later on, in the third stanza, it is more than evident that the agonized lover, the speaker, cannot redeem himself from the oppressive memory that is chiseled in his consciousness like a scorching spear. Hence, he keeps repeating and echoing the lamenting, mourning statement with which he commenced the poem:

"Our love has reached its termination."

Then he states the following:

"Pretty soon
The old, dull knives
Will be ready for a new battle of pain and spectacle."

The poem that commences with war-like images (defense walls which are breached; "brave") ends with war-like images ("knives"; "battle") while yielding a sense of circularity. The latter "encircles" the poem from both sides while reflecting metaphorically the war the speaker is "surrounded" by the oppressive recollections of his past, lost love.

And the knives? They are old and dull. Perhaps they were different in the past. Perhaps in the past, when the flame of the fervent love was still blazing, those knives were as sharp and as shrill as razors. And those sharp and shrill knives served the lovers in their battle. A battle that can be as blatantly bitter and even venomous as only a battle between past lovers can be. A battle that conceived and yielded the termination of their love. The pain of the past continues performing in the present but the tragedy ("tragic gesture" [tragic play]) will turn into a pallid, faded, feeble spectacle. Indeed, history does repeat, the first time as a tragedy and in the second time as a farce.

My Blood Dreamed Last Night about Your Blood

My blood dreamed last night about your blood
They both streamed together down the road
And our bodies were wide open like quarries
Stretched next to the cars. Quietly

Our white bodies were taken
Our merged blood was left, streaming.
It carried tiny chaff crumbs
While lingering slothfully, happily to the tunnel.

The one who rode at that time from Jerusalem
Thought that it was blood of one person, not of two.

The speaker experiences his emotional bond to his beloved woman in the most powerful fashion: his blood dreamed at night time about her blood. Undoubtedly, the connotations engaged with that image are remarkably positive: they reflect emotional closeness of the highest level possible. The following line develops and further cultivates the blood image:

"They both streamed together down the road."

The semantic character of this line is quite opaque: it seems that it amalgamates both positive and negative connotations. On the one hand, the connotations are still singularly positive: the merged blood continues radiating connotations of the strongest emotional closeness. On the other hand, however, streaming down the road, flowing down on the slope, is raged with negative connotations, associated with any kind of going down such as descent, decline, fall and degradation.

In the following two consecutive lines clean up that opacity:

"And our bodies were wide open like quarries
stretched next to the cars."

The positive, appealing connotations are muted while the negative connotations accumulate momentum, eclipse and silent the positive connotations and take over. The previous emotional closeness is indeed a deadly one. The blood of the speaker and his beloved woman merged as they were killed, next to each other, in a car accident. And when their white bodies were taken away from the accident's site, their merged blood continued streaming down the slope while carrying "tiny chaff crumbs." Describing the streaming, merged blood as carrying "tiny chaff crumbs" brings to mind a small brook streaming cheerfully. The unbridgeable gap between the deadly stream of blood and the cheerful stream of a brook further stresses the dreadful nature of the speaker's nightmare. In light of the above, the following, consecutive line is greatly enigmatic indeed:

> *"While lingering [the blood stream] slothfully, happily to the tunnel."*

Happily? Their merged blood is streaming happily after they got killed? Is it possible? The only plausible possibility is the following: Even at the moment of death, their unity reaches the very vertex of totality, the very zenith of wholeness, that only the word "happiness" can portray it.

> *"The one who rode at that time from Jerusalem*
> *Thought that it was blood of one person, not of two."*

The unity of the speaker and his beloved woman reaches its ultimate climax: they become one. Hence, like the sphinx, from whose ashes new life buds and sprouts, the death of both himself and of his beloved woman brings their unity to the most extreme vertex possible.

The Man Who Leaves

The man who leaves the woman whom he loved,
Will bounce his last word
Like a smooth stone bounced on the face of water
The stone will jump three times
Or perhaps even four. Then it will drown.

This very short poem consists of one image: when a man leaves a woman whom he loved in the past, his last word to her will be bounced like a stone which is bounced three or four times on the face of water before it drowns. Like in many love poems by Yehuda Amichai, love is frustrated love, broken, blemished, breached love. Unlike many other love poems by Yehuda Amichai, however, the speaker is not the hurt one, is not the deserted one. The speaker is the one who ripped and severed the love relations he had with his woman lover. Undoubtedly, he knows that his last word to her is "sentenced" to vanish like the stone bouncing on the face of water, is "doomed" to drown. Hence, why does he utter that last word? Does he still care about the woman whom he loved in the past and now he deserts her? Perhaps this is the way in which he verbally seals the "coffin" of their past love. Following that vein, it is not a love poem. It is a poem about shattered love that drowns like a stone in water, that is drowned by a man whose own heart turned as hard as a stone.

Love Technique No. 2

And there was evening and there was
morning: only six days
We were together, like the days of the world's creation
But in a reverse order,
We started with creating a happy man, later
We continued with creating animals, birds,
grass and all kinds of trees

And light
And we concluded with chaos and darkness
over an abyss.

From now on we will be compelled to create miracles
Each of us for himself only, like a person,
who by his own hands
Feeds, at night time, a vending machine with candies
So by next morning he will be encountered
By a click of a coin and by a metal knock, which are
A miracle of surprise.

And at night he will feed again the vending machine.

On the one hand, love is saturated with moving, heartfelt emotions. On the other hand, however, engaging love with a technique, yields an impression of an automatic, mechanical routine, one which is devoid of any emotions whatsoever. The latter is sadly manifested in most of the poem's second stanza.

The poem commences with a reflection to the six days in which the Universe was created by God, as narrated in the beginning of the Book of Genesis. Undoubtedly, the biblical story of the six-day creation is associated with the most positive, elevated connotations. Nevertheless, those positive, elevated connotations are challenged by the speaker, who laments that only six days were allocated for him and his beloved woman to be together.

Indeed, they launched their own creation process, although its unfolding order was the opposite of the one narrated in the Book of Genesis. Yet, the beginning of that reversed process of creation was certainly promising: "we started with creating a happy man..."

Yet, since the order of the creation process committed by the lovers inverses the order of the biblical creation process, it ends with the most negative, adverse connotation: Chaos, darkness, abyss. Hence, the promising commencement of the creation process executed by the lovers, is brutally clouded by its bleak, murky termination.

From the human perspective, the biblical creation seems like a miracle: the entire cosmos is created out of the void, out of vain emptiness. Now the lovers are forced to create their own miracles. They are like Adam and Eve who were evicted from the Garden of Eden and forced to build a new life on hostile, inimical, scalding soil. That and more.

The lovers in the poem are forced to face even a greater calamity: "Each of us for himself [and herself] only..." Hence, the lovers who experience such exceedingly short togetherness, whose fate reflects the exile of Adam and Eve from the Garden of Eden, are now sentenced to separation. Now they are doomed to be besieged by somber, scary solitude, by murky loneliness. So what is left for them?

The hounding, shadowing wretchedness of the pauper, of the impoverished hope of the poor: being like the needy who feeds, at night time, a vending machine, so in the morning, he will encounter both miracle and surprise.

And what are those miracle and surprise? A click of a coin, a dry, metal knock. This way the lovers are exiled from their shielding shelter of togetherness, from their soothing serenity, in order to encounter and experience the most pitiful surprise, the most miserable miracle.

Their only ally in the world is an automatic, metal heartless click. And even that click they are forced to experience separately. Only dust and ashes are left from their happy, loving togetherness. Bleak and murky is the world of the lovers who have been deprived of their love, who have been evicted from their love.

A Deserted House

A deserted house, one can easily tell that it is deserted
A deserted man, one cannot easily tell
that he is deserted
Since there is still light of memories in
his wide-open eyes.

A door is put upright in the middle of the field
Saying, here was a house
A thrown shoe on a thrown piece of cloth
Cannot tell that here was a man.

A woman is lamenting loudly: my beloved
My place, my beloved, my place
And a man is crying loudly, my wife, my house,
my house, my wife.

And perhaps we live in order to say "Five years ago"
"Twenty years ago," both are a solid shadow which
envelopes our fading life

A shadow and respect granted to our life,
a staff of pining for our old age.

The poem cultivates a cogent analogy between a house and a man: both are plagued by the touch of mortal termination, of death. However, while it is easy to discern the death of the house, its being deserted, it is not easy to tell that the man is dead: his eyes are wide open and there is a light of memories flickering in them. While memories belong to the past and the past is dead, it will never be revived, the flickering light in the wide open eyes of that man, heralds life, even *joie de vivre*. The deserted door in the field tells the sad story of the deserted house, of the life that once celebrated in that house but later vanished, turned into dust and ashes.

But why a thrown shoe and a thrown piece of cloth cannot testify that once they belonged to a man? Perhaps to stress how drastic was his morbid, deadly disappearance: Neither of them can attest to his past existence. No wonder that the following, consecutive stanza is wrought in the traditional form of the biblical lament, whose most typical literary character is the repetition:

"A woman is lamenting loudly: my beloved.
My place, my beloved, my place
And a man is crying loudly, my wife my house,
my house my wife."

Consider, for instance, the most famous lament that King David recites once he learns that Absalom, his son, got killed (while launching a rebellion against his own father, King David): "My son Absalom my son my son Absalom, if only I had died instead of you Absalom my son my son" (2 Samuel 19:1). And later: "The king covered his face and the king wept crying loud my son Absalom Absalom my son my son" (2 Samuel 19:5). And the following biblical lament:

"They shall not mourn for him
Oh my brother oh my sister
They shall not mourn for him
Oh master oh his majesty"

(Jeremiah 22:13)

And of course, Psalm 22:2: "My God, my God, why have you forsaken me" (as agonized Jesus cried on the cross).

The poem's fourth, concluding stanza is also touched by the cold, morbid presence of death. First, the lamenting tone about the years that fade away; and later, the sold shadow that may provide pining, support and even respect in our old age, but it can neither mute nor defeat death, which is lurking in ambush. No wonder that the poem is saturated with lamenting, mourning, wailing. And what about us? What is left for us?

Perhaps the words with which Yehuda Amicai concludes his very moving poem *Leah Goldberg Died*:

"Go in peace very wearied Leah
And what is left for us is only
Standing with our heads upright
While expecting tiding, bad and good
Interlaced in the scent of the pine trees."

Once I Bought a Mirror

Once I bought a mirror when my world shattered
Now the mirror shattered after my world
has been repaired
And the splinters of the shattered mirror
were thrown to the garbage.

This spring the first grass is sprouting on
the mountain's slope
Which was sliced to pave a road
This way the words follow immediately
the destruction
The last person who will ask "what was
Here under the grass?" Will keep silent

And what that happened will continue to happen.
Also prophecy is archaeology
At the end of words and time
A splinter of a shattered glass remains
standing upright

What is a mirror? What does a mirror do? And why did the poem's speaker need a mirror when his world shattered? A mirror reflects the image of the person who holds the mirror. For that very reason, the speaker needed a mirror, needed a mirror badly; his image reflected in the mirror told him that not his entire world shattered, that he still exists, that he does not look that bad, that hope is waiting for him beyond his murky, bleak present. Eventually, the world of the speaker has been repaired; he has met his remedy, he has encountered his redemption.

At that very point in the speaker's life point of relief and bliss, the mirror shattered. There is something very unfair about it: once the mirror has fulfilled its mission, after it bestowed upon the mourning speaker consolations, it shattered and its splinters were thrown to the garbage: "the moon has done his work, the moon may go." The mirror's service to the speaker was completed. It was not needed anymore. From now on it belonged to the garbage.

"This spring the first grass is sprouting on
the mountain's slope."

Undoubtedly, the sprouting—and eventually thriving—first grass of the spring heralds budding hope, promising future. The latter echoes the speaker's healing, his "resurrection." Also, this way a thematic-compositional hook of integration is woven between the poem's two stanzas. That hook is based on revival. That and more.

Another thematic-compositional hook of integration is interwoven between those two stanzas. Unlike the previous hook, however, this hook is based on negative destructive connotations: there is a reciprocal analogy between the shattered mirror and the mountain's sliced slope. In both cases the theme of ruining prevails. Hence, the previously cultivated optimistic connotations (the speaker's healing, the sprouting of the spring's first grass) are denied and removed as they are sadly replaced by somber connotations of demolition and eradication. Who is the last person who will ask: "What was/here under the grass?"

And isn't it more logical that he would ask: what was here under the paved road? And why he should keep silent? Isn't it more logical, more necessary, to protest against trapping, ruing the spring's first grass, against scaring and wounding brutally the mountain's slope, the beautiful nature?

The last person is the last one who witnessed how modern progress ruins nature. He is the last one who recalls the sprouting grass before it was devastated by a paved road. And he will ask what was under the grass as he fails to believe that is only the paved road that ravaged the spring's first thriving grass. He hopes to find a more humanistic reason, a more worthy reason that could justify (or at least explain) the destruction of the flourishing grass. And he should keep silent because there are no words, that can defend such an act of vandalism. As it is put by the prophet Amos: "At such a time the prudent man should keep silent" (Amos 5:13)

The poem's third and last stanza continues developing and cultivating the negative, disheartening, discouraging connotations while conferring upon them a philosophical touch: "And what which happened will continue to happen." Those words echo "piously" the pessimistic words of Kohelet: "what has happened is what will happen, what has occurred is what will occur. There is nothing new under the sun" (Kohelet [Ecclesiastes] 1:9).

Hence, the horizon is grim and gloomy: whatever a person may do is doomed to hopelessness. Human beings are sentenced to fate of futility, of despair. Whatever they may do, will make no difference, will change nothing, will improve nothing. They are trapped in a snare of nothingness. And why prophecy is archaeology? Since prophecy focuses on the future and archaeology focuses on the past, if prophecy is archaeology, the future echoes the past, the past echoes the future, and both of them are captured in the same timeless snare. Both past and present are robbed of their unique characteristics: nothing is meaningful anymore, everything is erased, scraped, blotted. And only time, like a somber bird of prey, hovers over the void. "*Tempus edax rerum*": Time devours everything.

The poem that commences with splinters of a shattered mirror (which is made of glass) reaches its termination with a splinter of a shattered glass:

> *"At the end of words and time*
> *A splinter of a shattered glass remains*
> *standing upright."*

Words have reached their end. Time has reached its end. Nothing is left. Indeed, not quite so. In a wordless world, in a world where (as the prophet Amos puts it) the prudent man should keep silent, in such a world, time will continue endlessly to hover over the void. It has been already stated: the analogy between the splinters of the shattered mirror with which the poem commences and the splinters of the shattered glass with which the poem concludes, yield a sense of circularity. That circularity stresses and reinforces the profound meaning of that analogy. That analogy is based on injustice.

After the mirror served well the poem's speaker, it is treated unjustly by throwing its splinters to the garbage. The injustice associated with splinter of the shattered glass at the conclusion of the poem. However, is of colossal, cosmic, existential nature: the injustice done to human beings by caging them in a world which is devoid of hope, of capacity to change, to improve.

The splinter of the shattered glass, stuck upright on what may be an archeological mound, brings to mind a tombstone. Unlike the mirror, the glass is transparent. This way one can see through the glass. Yet, cruel irony is lurking: there is nothing but emptiness that can be seen through this glass: nothing but the very vertex of void. So what is left? Nothing is left. Beside that glass tombstone which is beyond time, beyond human hope.

A Spring Poem

Because of hesitations
Between, March and April, a happy
Space was created

The world is like the moment in which
The loved woman is digging in her purse
Looking for her door's key.
Suddenly a ring is heard from a rustle of papers:
Here it is!

This short poem consists of a tense, colossal gap between something of enormous, majestic measurements and something of tiny, minute measurements: between the year's seasons and a door's key.

In the first stanza, a gap is created between March and April. That gap is a happy one since it is yielded due to hesitations practiced upon the transition from one season to the following one, between March and April. The happiness of that gap derives from those hesitations since there is something very vulnerable, benevolence, human, in lack of decisiveness, lack of absoluteness.

Also in the second stanza there is a gap. This gap, however, is far from being a colossal one. This gap is a trifling gap, a gap between looking for a key (by the beloved woman) in a purse and finding the key. The ending of each of the two stanzas produces a feeling of relief, generates a feeling of deliverance: a creation of a happy space in the first stanza, finding the misplaced key in the second stanza.

In both cases, the "happy punch line" produces an optimistic atmosphere, atmosphere of ease, which is translated in the conclusion of the second stanza into a delicate touch of humor. No wonder that the poem is entitled "*A Spring Poem.*" Spring is associated with the most positive, optimistic, promising connotations. Those connotations are conceived by this poem to their idealistic fullest.

He Left

"He left two sons" it is commonly said
About a man who died. Sometimes when
he is still alive.

An echo of great love that vanished, is like the echo
Of a bark of a big dog in an empty house in Jerusalem
Which is sentenced to be destroyed.

The entire poem heralds the somber message of loss, bereavement and death: death of a man, death of love. When a man dies, he leaves nothing but his offspring. Even if he created innovatively, prolifically, even if he established an admirable project, articulated and delivered commendable speeches, his death is of such a total magnitude that it seems to yield nothing but void, to sentence all his accomplishments to forgotten dust and ashes.

Indeed, reality teaches us differently. Many achievements and accomplishments reached in the past life of a person who died (like written books, works of art, architecture, inventions, theories and much more) continue living after the death of a man who created them.

Yet, this is the despairing, bleak, and murky perspective of the poem's speaker. That speaker continues by saying the following: sometimes it can be said ("he left two sons") about a person who is still alive. In such a case, that person (or man, as it is put in the poem) has accomplished nothing in his life, has created nothing in his life. He was already dead when he was still alive.

The poem's second stanza narrates the equally despairing story of love that died. Like in the case of the dead man: even if that love was once fervently kindled, nothing of that fervidly ignited love is left after it extinguished. Nothing. Only an echo of a dog in a desolate house which is sentenced to be ravaged.

This is a poem that introduces a grim, gloomy, mournful philosophy about the hopeless futility of life, about the helplessness of human beings upon being doomed to die, upon being sentenced to be void and forgetfulness. From dust to dust. From ashes to ashes.

Late in My Life

Late in my life I come to you
Sifted through many doors, diminished on stains.
Almost nothing is left of me.

And you, such a surprised woman, an animal
of half courage
A wild woman with eye glasses, the elegant
harness of your eyes.

"Things like to get lost and be found again
By other people; only people like
To find themselves". That is what you said.

Later you bisected your perfect face
Into two profiles, one for distance
And one for me as a memento and then you left.

The poem's speaker comes to his past beloved woman late in his life: after all his previous loves, after all his previous life experiences, exhausted in his mind and body, reduced and lessened in his very existence. He has become a faint, frail, faded shadow himself.

No wonder that his past beloved woman is surprised. As if she is asking him: Now? Are you coming to me now? Like that? This way? So poorly deteriorated? So declined? And do you expect me to take you back? Like that?

The speaker, however, humbled by his past beloved woman's rebuking attitude (indeed, an assumed one) portrays her while utilizing animal like terms (which are in full congruence with her assumed blatantly brutal attitude). He calls her "an animal of half courage", he calls her eye glasses "an elegant harness" and he calls her "a wild woman." But why "an animal of half courage"? Why only "half courage"?

Perhaps because she is not entirely an animal. And for that very reason he describes her eye glasses as "an elegant harness." A harness is associated with a domesticated, tamed animal (like a horse) and "elegant" is associated with a woman. Hence, the past beloved woman is half woman, half like an animal, like the legendary centaur in Greek mythology which is half man (woman, in this case) and half horse (mare, in this case).

In the third stanza, the woman beloved says the following to her past desperate lover, the poem's speaker:

"Things like to get lost and be found again
By other people; only people like
To find themselves "That is what you said,"

The scolding irony practiced by the past woman beloved could not be more blatantly piercing.

Since the lost speaker comes to her "to find himself," to resurrect his "ramshackle" life, he is like "things" according to her statement. He is not like "people" who "like to find themselves." The speaker, according to her statement, is nothing but a "thing" since he needs her shielding, sheltering support to find himself. The way the past beloved woman scorns and mocks the speaker could not be more bitterly biting.

"Later you bisected your perfect face
Into two profiles, one for distance
And one for me as a memento and then your left."

As Greek mythology is previously "enlisted" (centaur) now Roman mythology is "enlisted." The bisected face of the past woman beloved echoes the ancient Roman god Janus, who has two faces: one is facing the past, the other is facing the future. One profile of the bisected face of the past beloved woman is facing the distance. The distance is her future. And the speaker has no access to her future.

The second profile is nothing but a memento which she gives the loving speaker before leaving him. Nothing can be more pitiful, more humiliating than leaving a memento to a desperate, hopeless lover, whose heart is broken and whose mind is dispirited. Upon his part, love does not live here anymore. Who knows? Perhaps never did.

Shifra and Batya

Shifra and Batya ensured in their
Thighs eternal youth.

Such fresh years of birth
Fill their thighs with tense sweetness
And fill my brain with a tone that is like a bright string.

They said: men are strange and senseless:
They decorate a sword which is made to kill
With engraving and pearals

But the organ that grants joy
They don't decorate at all.

Shifra is a biblical name. Biblical Shifra (with Poua) was the midwife who disobeyed Pharaoh's atrocious command to murder all male newborns (Exodus 1:15-20). This way, using the name Shifra in the poem yields desirable connotations of life, compassion, and loving-kindness. The name Batya, despite its religious meaning ("daughter of God") is not biblical. Yet, the name Bithia is biblical. In 1 Chronicles 4:18, we read about the daughter of Pharaoh, whose name was Bithia. That and more.

In the book of Exodus (2:6-10) the daughter of Pharaoh is also connected to life and compassion: she took pity on the Hebrew baby whom she called Moses (Moshe), kept him alive despite her father's murderous command and raised him like her own son. Hence, all those connotations of life are echoed loud and clear by the sensuality of Shifra and Batya, by their engagement with “eternal youth” and “fresh years of birth. And nothing can herald better their sensuality than their “thighs” and the “tense sweetness” of their “thighs.” Hence, it is their abounding sensuality, their flowing sexuality, that meet perfectly the connotations of life which are invested in the poem.

The speaker draws overwhelming pleasure from their plentiful sensuality and sexuality to the point that he feels that his brain turns into a musical instrument that produces a tone that is like a bright string. It is a matter of interest that he does not relate to his heart, the traditional center of emotions while relating to his brain the traditional center of rational faculties, which are devoid of emotional inclinations. However, Shifra’s and Batya’s sensuality and sexuality are so powerfully overwhelming to the point that they penetrate even the speaker’s bodily organ, which is traditionally disengaged from emotions.

The bountiful sensuality and sexuality of Shifra and Batya cause them to wonder how come that men decorate their swords, the source of killing and death and not their sexual organs, the source of life and pleasure. This poem is a salute to the very vertex of life and joie de vivre.

Once Great Love

Once great love bisected my life into two slices
And the first slice continues convulsing
In another place, like an amputated snake.
The passing years have soothed me
And have conferred remedy upon my heart
and comfort upon my eyes.

And I am like a man who is standing in
the Judea desert
Facing a sign that says "sea level".
This way I remember your face everywhere
At your face level.

Like most of love poems by Yehuda Amichai, also this poem unfolds the hurting, touching story of broken, breached love, love that is marked by pain and pining, scalding frustrations and scorching sears.

The poem commences with following confession by the poem's speaker:

"Once great love bisected my life into two slices"

Indeed, it was not love that bisected the speaker's life into two slices but rather his being rejected, evicted from his beloved's life, that severed severely his life. Hence, the speaker avoids (perhaps unconsciously) the blatantly bitter truth, the fact that his beloved cast him off her life since he cannot tolerate such piercingly heartbreaking truth.

The same "denial technique" practiced by the emotionally defeated speaker is clearly displayed in his following proclamation:

"And the first slice continues convulsing
In another place, like an amputated snake".

In another place? That slice of his bisected life continues convulsing in another place? Indeed, the speaker continues looking for a refuge from the disheartening truth in the bosom of misleading illusion. Hence, the slice that continues convulsing is not convulsing "in another place" but rather in the very place of the speaker. Thus, when the truth is too painful for the speaker to cope with, he is looking for a shielding shelter of a deceitful belief.

"The passing years have soothed me
And have conferred remedy upon my heart and
comfort upon my eyes".

Have passing years truly soothed him? Have passing years truly conferred remedy upon his heart and comfort upon his eyes? Indeed, he is the one who uses the present tense—and not the past tense!—upon portraying the one slice of his bisected life that continues (not continued!) convulsing like an amputated snake.

That and more. The next concluding stanza of the poem plausibly demonstrates how the speaker is painfully far from being soothed by the passing years, from finding remedy and experiencing comfort.

"And I am like a man who is standing
in the Judean desert
Facing a sign that says "sea level"
This way I remember your face everywhere
At your face level."

Although he does not see his beloved, her memory is engraved in his recollection like a mordant, searing scar, like an open, bleeding wound. He may deny it as fervently as he may desire: Yet, no soothing comfort is awaiting him. He is doomed to his hounding pain, he is sentenced to his spearing, piercing somber destiny. He is harnessed to that suffocating, stabbing destiny, painful far from even a minute sliver of relief. Forever he is evicted from the pampering soothing bosom of comfort.

Late Quiet Happiness

I am standing in a place where once I loved.
Rain is falling. The rain is my home.

I think in words of longing,
Words of a landscape to the end of capacity.

I remember you waiving your hand,
As if wiping white vapor of a window.

And your face looks enlarged
Like taken from an old, blurry photograph.

Once I did great injustice
To myself and to other people.

But the world is shaped nicely and is built well, and is
Built for rest, like a bench in a public boulevard.

And I found in my life
Late, quiet happiness

Like severe illness which is diagnosed late:
A little more time for tranquil happiness.

Also this poem, like many love poems by Yehuda Amichai, is about love that faded away, love that met its termination. Yet, unlike in many Amichai's poems about frustrated, breached love, it is not quite clear that the speaker is the one who is "victimized" by the collapse of that love. Indeed, he is painfully far from celebrating the crush, the thrashing of that love. However, it seems that he is also responsible for the loitering, the slump of that love.

Already in the first line of the poem, the speaker says that the separation (caused by the collapse of the love) was not forced on him: "I am standing in a place where once I loved". Since "once he [I] loved" means that he does not love anymore, that his love reached its termination, the termination of that love was not forced on him by his rejecting , denying female lover.

"Rain is falling. The rain is my home".

The falling rain is a metaphor for erasing the past, wiping out the past, eradicating and expunging the love that was a prominent part of that past. Now the past is gone. Now the love is gone.

No wonder that the speaker, the past lover, declares loud and clear: "The rain is my home". The erasing, eradicating rain is his home; the rain which converts the past love into a non existing entity is his home, the rain that smudges and blots the love of his past is his home.

"I think in words of longing
Words of a landscape to the end of capacity".

This second, consecutive stanza, seems to partially contest the previous one. Apparently, the lost love that seemed to sink in the distant misty past, is not that lost after all: it still ignites the speaker's longing, it still kindles his pinings and yearnings. He still thinks in "words of a landscape to the end of capacity: this is the landscape of his recollections, recollections which are stretched "to the end of capacity": the end of the capacity to recall, to revive memories of the past love, to resurrect reminiscences of seemingly forgotten feelings:

"I remember you waiving your hand,
As if wiping white vapor of a window".

Now a memory starts surfacing. However the loving gesture (waving a hand for signaling either hello or so long) is "contaminated," "soiled" by being compared with a meaningless, loveless gesture, such as wiping white vapor of a window. Hence, what could be considered an act of love is portrayed in terminology of a mundane, dull, banal activity.

"And your face looks enlarged
Like taken from an old, blurry photograph."

Again, the past casts a clouding shade on the recollection: the vital vividness of what a new the present is already eclipsed by that very present.

"Once I did great injustice
To myself and to other people".

Hence, the first impression that the speaker has not been victimized by a rejecting female lover earns further confirmation: he is the one who did injustice, not only to himself but to other people as well. Yet, the poem ends with a touch of comfort, of consolation:

"But the world is shaped nicely and is
built well, and is
Built for rest, like a bench in a public boulevard".

The following, final stanza of the poem seems to continue cultivating the very same rhetoric of soothing consolation:

"And I found in my life
Late quiet happiness
Like severe illness which is diagnosed late
A little more time for quiet happiness."

The last two sentences shrewdly refute and deny the very essence of the previously introduced consolation: the late quiet happiness is nothing but a misleading surface that conceals morbid, terminal illness, one that leaves only "A little more time for quick happiness".

Thus, the poem "fails" to deliver, it "fails" to fulfill its soothing, consoling, comforting "gospel". But that "failure" is nothing but a skillfully, aesthetic dexterity that bestows upon the poem its rewarding touch of artistic sophistication.

Nobody

Nobody puts his trust in me.
Dreams of other people are barred for me.
I have no place in them

Also the sounds of speaking in the room
Are a sign of desolation like a spider's web.

The loneliness of the body
Leaves enough room for other bodies.

Removing the loves one by one,
From the shelf, until it becomes empty

And the external space commences.

The poem seems to reflect the feelings of void upon the part of the speaker, feelings which are the very vertex of emptiness, of nothingness, of blank. Nobody puts his trust in the speaker as if the speaker does not exist on is not worth of being trusted. Naturally, the level of his self-confidence could not be lower, could not be more depressed. He is evicted not only from the lives of other people. He is exiled from the dreams of other people. Wherever he goes, he encounters blocking bars, wired barricades of rejection, denial and refusal. No welcome sign has ever been drawn for him. Even when he hears sounds of conversing in the room, for him they are nothing but a sign of negligence, or desertion, of desolation, like a spider's web. Human voices sound strange and alien to him.

The loneliness of his body makes his body so shrunk, so diminished, to the point that it leaves room to more bodies. Under such circumstances, circumstances of loneliness, unworthiness and despair, even loves, the most precious, priceless assets, turn worthless. One by one, they are removed from the shelf, until the shelf turns totally empty. As if loves have never lived on it, surely never will.

And the emptiness of the shelf, the shelf from which all loves have been exiled and expelled, already heralds the external, empty space. Space which is marked by arctic nothingness, space which is marked by murky, bleak darkness, space which is marked by endless lifelessness. And this is the space of the speaker. A space from which feelings have migrated. A space devoid of love. A space in which loves are like old suitcases, removed from the shelf, one by one, for one way trip. A trip with no return. And there is nothing sadder than a one-way trip, than a trip with no return.

Love Technique No. 6

Love is time infusion: when a man and a woman
lie together
At night, they are filled with time which they
lost during the day.

This singularly tiny poem consists of one simile: The very definition of love, the very essence of love, is like infusion of time: when a man and a woman lie together at night time, it is like they are infused with time which they lost during daytime. The following questions must surface: How did they lose time during daytime? What caused them to lose time during the unfolding day?

Those questions lead and direct us to one answer. During the daytime, they were not together, their time of togetherness was deprived of them, was robbed of them. For that reason they need a time infusion during the night to reinforce their togetherness, to compensate for the togetherness time that was plundered from them during the slowly unfolding day. So much emotional tenderness, so much moving loving—kindness in two poetic lines only.

Last Leaf

The last leaf that dropped represented the entire tree
One word replaced your entire body

A leaf stuck to my show. And I did not know.
Your word is touching my heart. And I did not know.

The first stanza obtrusively displays a theme of termination, of separation: the last leaf that dropped (and this way represented the entire tree) and the last word (probably uttered by the female beloved prior to deserting her lover, the rejected longing, hurting speaker) represents her entire yearned body. Hence, even one tiny metonym is enough to ignite and kindle the recollections of the distant, misty past. And in the case of the last uttered word, that distant, misty past is painfully far from being both misty and distant: it continues haunting, shadowing, and tormenting the rejected lover's/speaker's very present.

Indeed, both the fallen last leaf and last uttered word continue hounding the deserted lover/speaker: the last falling leaf is stuck to his shoe and his rejecting beloved's last word is stabbing his heart. In both cases (the last leaf which is stuck to his shoe; her last word which is touching his heart)

The line concludes with the following two Hebrew words: *veloh edah*, which literally mean "and I will not know." That Hebrew expression is to be traced in three Biblical contexts (very different from each other): Isaiah, 47:8: "And I will know no bereavement"; Job 9:21 : "I am flawless and I will not know my soul"; Psalms 100:4: "I will know no evil".

The expression "and I will not know" in the two concluding lines of this poem, however, may be understood as follows: I have been moved profoundly by the fall of the last leaf and by the last word to the point that my heart cannot contain anymore my overflowing feelings. In light of the above, that biblical expression which repeats twice at the very conclusion of the poem turns the bitter taste of termination that prevails through the unfolding continuum of the poem into a heartening touch of gentle emotionality.

The Doors Are Shut

The shut doors were expected
To be always open for me. And the doors
which I can open
Guard empty places
Like ancient graves that had been looted.

I think about love of people
Who forgot to take off the decorations
after the holiday:
What has been left for them?

So long, you too, my love. The hour
In which we wake up to separate
Has been fixed inside me, like in an alarm clock

That does not have to wake up anymore, and it only
Produces a sound of a dry knock.

The first stanza propounds feelings of disappointment, despondency, dejection: those doors which have been always expected to be open and inviting for me are now shut, barred and barricaded. And the doors which I can still open guard nothing but emptiness, like the ancient graves of kings that had been robbed and plundered.

The feel of emptiness, even of worthlessness, keeps echoing in the second stanza while being connected, this time, to the absence of love. If nothing is left of the love of people who forgot to take off the holiday decorations, it means that that love was devoid of real value, was like an empty shell to begin with. That love was as dated, as faded, as forgotten and neglected as old holiday decorations.

The third, last, and concluding stanza of the poem presents the theme of empty worthless love from a new angle. That angle is the last, final separation of the lovers. The lovers set an alarm clock before launching a trip (by one of them) that will lead to their final and total separation. The alarm clock will not ring, will not wake up anymore, however. It will produce nothing but a dry, dead knock.

The lovers are gone. The love is gone. No alarm clock in the world will wake up that dead love. That dead love is as dead as the shut, barred barricaded doors. That dead love is as dead as the empty, looted, ancient graves. That dead love is as dead as the faded, forgotten holiday decorations.

That dead love is as dead as a dead alarm clock. That dead love is dead. Period. And nobody can bring it back to life.

Remembering is a Kind of Hope

The speed of the distance between us:
It is not that one already left and the other one stayed,
It is the double speed of those who go away
from each other.

From the house which I demolished, even the
splinters are not mine,
And once the words which we wanted to say
to each other
During our lives together
Are like a precise pile of windows grouped
next to a new building
When we still kept silent

I don't know what happened to you since then
As I don't know what happened
To me since then!
Remembering is a kind of hope.

Like so many love poems by Yehuda Amichai—also in this poem—love is breached, splintered, fractured. The two lovers are hopelessly separated. An emotional stumbling block is erected between them, a fiery abyss keeps them away from each other. The speaker confesses; he demolished the house that belonged to both of them. Because of his violent destructiveness, their protective shielding shelter, the one that nourished and cultivated their love, turned into ash, ramshackle, rickety ruins.

And he further confesses; even the crashed splinters of that ruined house are not his anymore. The alienation radiated by that crushed house (the one which the speaker/lover built himself shattered) the house that shielded and sheltered their love, could not be more blatantly bitter.

And what about words, words exchanged between the speaker and his beloved? Those words have never been uttered. Those words have been as mute, as speechless "as a precise pile of windows grouped next to a new building/ when we still kept silent".

The theme of a window prevails in many poems by Yehuda Amichai. A window symbolizes openness, vastness, broadness, limitless, promising horizons, optimism, faith in the future. In this poem, however, the windows are not installed in their right places: they are placed in a pile, obviously useless, obviously devoid of their capacity to fulfill their promising, optimistic symbolization.

The title of the poem is "Remembering is a kind of Hope." Such is also the concluding line of the poem. Yet, in the third, last stanza of the poem the speaker/lover confesses that he does not know what happened to his beloved (after their separation) nor does he know what happened to him. Hence, his "remembering mechanism" is sadly impaired, regretfully blemished. If remembering is a kind of hope, he is desperately robbed of hope. And since his house was a symbol of his (and his beloved's) love, love does not live here anymore.

Poems About Tolerating Life: Between Pain and Pining

A Man Standing Next to a Window

A man is standing next to a window
and raising his hands.
He will not travel anymore. He will travel.
He will not travel.
Help him to put in order his belongings.
He is haunted by dates. Fold for him
His suit, his atonement, in a suitcase.
He will always leave pictures on the wall of his room.

A man next to a window is raising his hands.
When does he get his food,
His conjugal nights, the days of his death?
What does he want? Look, what kind of thoughts
Are sailing around him, like ships, looking for a
Directed, convenient place for an eternal anchorage.

A man who set next to a window shut the window.
Because he will travel. He will not travel.
Don't help him. He will travel.

Like in other poems by Yehuda Amichai, the window symbolizes openness, new horizons, new promising possibilities, hope, desirable wishes, optimism, yearning, aspiration. A man who is standing next to a window, symbolizes his readiness to experience all those promising, gratifying possibilities. This man, however, is raising his hands. A person raises his hands not for saying either "hello" or "so long." For such greeting, a person raises one hand only. Thus, a man raises his two hands to convey this way a humble, meek, submissive message of either giving in or giving up. Such capitulation, such submission, reflects perfectly well that man's behavior and attitude throughout the entire poem.

He is preparing for a trip. He is not preparing for a trip. He opens a suitcase while demonstrating this way his wish to launch his trip, to embark on experiencing new life, new promising hopes, new gratifying possibilities. Yet, he leaves the pictures on the wall, which means that he intends to stay.

He shuts the window, which means he shuts the window for new life, new promising, rewarding possibilities, new gratifying horizons. He is weak. He is hesitant. He is fickle. Undependable. Inconsistent. He is surrounded by thoughts that said, like ships, around him; he is besieged by contradictory, conflicting thoughts; he is torn by confusing, perplexing, muddling thoughts that lead him to nowhere, that erect on his way of life stumbling blocks which he fails to overcome.

He is doomed to his weakness; he is sentenced to his feebleness. He needs someone who will help him to navigate his faint life, that will serve for him as a compass that will lead his unstable life to a harbor of refuge. The poem's speaker is approaching an anonymous man, instructing him to guide and coach that helpless man, to put his life in order, even to fold neatly his clothes in a suitcase. It is a matter of considerable interest that some words inlaid along the poem's textual continuum are borrowed from ancient Jewish textual sources: "*chalifato*", "*kparato*", "*mezono*", "*onato*", "*Chalifato*" ("his period"]; borrowed from the Bible); "*Caparato*" ("his atonement"; borrowed from the "*siddur*" [the Jewish prayer book]); "*mezono*" ("his food"; borrowed from the "*ketuba*" (the Jewish marriage certificate); "*onato*" ("his period"; borrowed from both the Bible and the "Ketuba", relating to the wife's —not husband's— conjugal rights).

Those "ancient" words bestow upon the poem a "philosophical" depth, following Kohelet (Ecclesiastes): There is nothing new under the sun" (Ibid. 1:9).

And why is that man haunted by dates? Because dates are anchored in the past, engaged with events that happened in the past, and by being chained to the past that man shuts the window for the future. This way he exiles himself from the promise of the future while he continues trampling in the bog of his hounding indecisiveness, his shadowing frailty. Amen.

The Estimate of Distances

I have lost the estimate of distances mastered by a cat
Which springs from roof to roof
I keep pondering and calculating
While falling down and hunting myself

My interactions with people have turned harder
And they are shattered easily.
The one who cannot quarrel with a peddler
in the market
Cannot love all over again

The longer I live, the more pains I am
compelled to collect
In order to experience a miracle, or at least
A surprise
Like experiencing upon using an automatic
vending machine
Which is fed by a lonely, sad man
At night.

This is a sad poem. This is a poem about a man who has lost the desirable capacity to be spontaneous, courageous, daring, resilient, adaptable, being able to cope innovatively, creatively, with reality, notably with changing, challenging reality. Losing a touch of worthy spontaneity, he keeps calculating and calculating, yet he continuously falls down, he continuously fails. And all those falls and failures are both frustrating and painful.

His unfortunate lack of spontaneity is further demonstrated through his reciprocal communications with people: his communications are rigid, unbending, hardened, and they fail easily.

What does the speaker mean by stating that "The one who cannot quarrel with a peddler in the market cannot love all over again"? For both—quarreling with a peddler and loving again—a person needs courage, resilience, determined capacity to cope with challenging, testing reality, to accommodate new rules of action, to give up one kind of code and embrace a new kind of code, to adjust oneself to changing reality.

Time is not an ally of the speaker. The older he turns, the more demanding efforts he is compelled to invest in order to encounter a miracle or at least a surprise. But what kind of a miracle? And what kind of a surprise? Regretfully, both are the most pathetically meek commodities: The same miracle, the same surprise, that a sad, lonely man's experiences upon emptying an automatic vending machine that he himself fed the night before.

As previously noted—a sad poem.

Neither tragic nor heartbreaking. Simply sad.

A Man Standing Next to a River With Fog

The white, merciful fog
Shuts his eyes
Like a black kerchief that covers the
Eyes of the man who is about to be executed

*And his cry, "Where are you?"**
Echoes the cry "Vive la liberté"!
Heard in heroic days which already faded away.

*feminine

This poem consists of two parts. Indeed, one may cogently argue the following: the poem is constructed in a fashion of a literary simile in which the main part (like a tenor in a metaphor) is the man whose eyes are shut by the white, merciful fog and the secondary part (like a vehicle in a metaphor) is the executed man (probably French) whose eyes are covered by a black kerchief.

Who is this man whose eyes are shut by the white, merciful fog? That man remains unknown. However, one thing is clear: like the executed man, he is also doomed, he is also sentenced to death. The fact that the fog (which is rising from the river as hinted by the poem's title) is both white and merciful does not change the fatal, deadly destiny of that man.

The poem provides hints that elucidate the circumstances of the "vehicle," the poem's secondary part: being executed while his eyes are shut by a black kerchief; his cry "*Vive la liberté*"; the reference to "heroic days"—all are hints to the French Revolution.

Indeed, from a factual perspective, the fate of the man whose eyes are shut by the white, merciful fog, is quite opaque. Yet, his comparison to the executed man, the portrayal of the fog as "merciful" (like a merciful nurse), his desperate cry to his loved woman—all lead to the conclusion that his comparison to the executed man is a robust one.

Indeed, the deadly circumstances of the executed man (the vehicle) are brutal and crude and the deadly circumstances of the man who is enveloped by the "pacifying" touch of the white, merciful fog, are "soothing." Yet, death, is death, is death, is death.

It is said in the context of the executed man that the heroic days already faded away. It is more than probable that the days of the man in the white, merciful fog were not heroic. Yet, they equally faded away. And his desperate cry—"Where are you?"— met no response.

The Place Where We Are Right

In the place where we are right
Flowers will never grow
In the spring.

The place where we are right
Is hard and trampled
Like a pressed yard.

But doubts and loves
Make the world softly crumbled
Like a mole, like ploughing
And a whisper will be heard in a place
Where there was a house
That was destroyed.

The poem is comprised of three stanzas and each stanza heralds a declaration. Indeed, the declarations heralded in the poem's first two stanzas echo each other, while the declaration heralded in the poem's third, concluding stanza stems from the nature of the previously heralded two declarations.

Why will flowers never grow in the place where we are right? And why the place where we are right is hard and trampled like a pressed yard? There is one answer for those questions. The feeling of rightness does not leave room for other feelings; the feeling of rightness clouds and mutes all other feelings; the feeling of rightness is a dam, is a barrier, is a stumbling block that blocks and suffocates all other feelings. The feeling of rightness yields and produces undesirable rigidity, one that suffocates worthy flexibility. For that very reason, flowers will never grow in the spring in the place where we are right and for that very reason, the place where we are right is as hard and trampled as a pressed yard.

As the Hebrew adage puts it critically: Let there be justice (rightness) regardless the pain it may cause (literally: "Let justice/rightness pierce the mountain.")

Or as it was poetically put by Nathan Alterman, the highly renowned Hebrew/Israeli poet in one of the numerous stanzas of his series of poems entitled *The Poems of the Plagues of Egypt*:

Although the judgment of the javelin is right
Wherever it prevails while bleeding
It always leaves a taste of salt
Like the tear of the innocent.

Perhaps we are right. Perhaps rightness is on our side. But there is always the one who pays the bitter price.

So what is the desirable alternative? What is the aspired solution? The following are the desirable alternative, the aspired solution: doubts love, flexibility, adaptability, easiness, pliancy. Everything that makes the soil of the world as crumbled and soft as it became after being ploughed, after being diligently dug by a field mole.

Indeed, once there was a house. And the house was demolished, was ruined. And in Yehuda Amichai's poetry, a ravaged house quite often symbolizes ravaged love. In this poem, however, the destruction of the house is not a total one. A whisper is heard in the place where the house used to be. And where there is a whisper there is hope. And a whisper, unlike a cry, goes well with flexibility, with easiness, with crumbled, ploughed soil, with doubts, with love. With hope. Hence, the poem that commences with undesirable, rigid rightness, prudently concludes with aspired flexibility and softness. In other words: with closeness, with love.

To Forget a Person

To forget a person is like
To forget to turn off the light in the yard
And the light remains on also during the day:
But it is also to remember
By the light.

This short poem consists of the tense contradictory relations between remembering and forgetting. And also: between light and darkness. The poem commences with the following statement:

"To forget a person is like
To forget to turn off the light in the yard
And the light remains on also during the day."

To forget to turn off the light in the yard during daytime (after it was on all night long) is truly quite elementary. Such a thing happens frequently while possessing no significance whatsoever. Thus, is it so elementary, so simple to forget a person as the poem's speaker suggest? Indeed, it is not. And the poem's speaker explains: leaving the light on (in the yard) also during day time it means to remember (a person) also thanks to the light that was left on.

The latter brings to mind a memorial candle which is lit in order to commemorate a person who left the land of the living. This way, the elementary, daily, banal act of forgetting to turn off the night light in the yard during daytime, goes through metaphorical metamorphosis: it becomes a tender act of longing and remembrance. Hence, forgetfulness is converted into touching commemoration.

Windows and Graves

There are many windows in my life
And many graves

Sometimes they change
Roles:
At that time a window is shut for good,
And through the tombstone
I can see
For distance.

Prior to discussing the way the window theme (openness, vastness, hope, promise for the future, optimistic expectations) is used in the poem's first stanza, let us focus on the prudent, effective fashion in which the dynamic nature of the text is utilized in the poem's first stanza.

It was Lessing in his celebrated book *Laoocon* (1766) who described literature as art of temporal medium (like music, dance, drama, unlike those of spatial medium [painting, sculpture] in which the textual components are inlaid in sequence. This way, in any work of literature (poetry, prose fiction [novel, story], play), the textual components reciprocally interact with each other. In this way, all thos mediums of art are temporal; it takes time to experience them.

That reciprocal interaction consists of the following three types of interaction. Those three types of reciprocal interaction are dictated and conditioned by the way the later bulk component of textual information affects the way in which the reader comprehends the earlier bulk of literary information.

Hence, there are three types of such reciprocal interaction between the early bulk component of textual information (inlaid along the textual continuum) and the late bulk of textual information (inlaid along the textual continuum).

The first type is the simplest: the late bulk of textual information joins the early bulk of textual information without changing at all the way the reader previously comprehended the early bulk of textual information.

In the second type of reciprocal interaction between both kinds of bulk of textual information, the late bulk of textual information moderately changes the way the reader previously comprehended the early bulk of textual information. In such a case, the reader has to practice "reverse reading," to go back to the early bulk of textual information, and reread it, this time in light of the "elucidating," "updating" late bulk of textual information.

The third type of the reciprocal interaction between the two kinds of textual information is the most drastic, dramatic one. In such a case, the late bulk of textual information casts the most rigorous, new light upon the early bulk of textual information. Hence, the reader is compelled to perform a drastic reverse reading, and this time neglects entirely his/her previous comprehension of the early bulk of textual information and replaces it with a completely new comprehension, one that is dictated by the later bulk of textual information.

Poetry often uses such a reciprocal interaction between early and late bulks of textual information. In such cases, poetry creates lack of congruence between the line unit and the syntactical unit. Thus the sentence (the syntactical unit) does not end where the line ends and it "slides down" and continues in the next, consecutive line. Sometimes, however, the sentence does not end even in that next, consecutive line, and it continues "sliding down" to the following line. And sometimes the entire poem consists of one sentence, one syntactical unit, that keeps "gliding down" from the poem's first line to the poem's last line. Such a literary phenomenon is called "run-on-line" (In French: *enjambement*; in Hebrew: *glishah / psichah*).

Indeed, the "run-on-line" makes the only difference between poetry and prose fiction. Metaphors, similes, metonyms, structured rhythm, meter, rhyme, which are traditionally associated with poetry, may be also traced in prose fiction (see, for instance, the case of "stream of consciousness" prose fiction like *Ulysess* by James Joyce).

However, only in poetry does the poet dictate the length of the text's line for aesthetically oriented reasons while in prose fiction, the publisher (and not the author!) dictates the length of the text's lines for practical, economical reasons (which format of the book is more economically useful to be produce, which format of the book may sell better, which length of the text's lines is more easily readable, etc.).

All the above leads to the first stanza of *Windows and Graves*, one that uses run-on-line both prudently and effectively.

There are many windows in my life
And many graves.

It has been already stated: a window in the poetry of Yehuda Amichai symbolizes promising horizons, hope, optimistic expectations, positive aspirations, good wishes. Hence, the poem's opening line, the one that proclaims many windows in the life of the speaker, could not be more optimistic, more promising. However, at this point, the text practices a "run-on-line": the sentence does not end at the end of the line, it "slides down" to the next, consecutive line, and reads as follows:

"And many graves"

The optimism and hope of the poem's first, opening line could not be contradicted in a more blatantly bitter way. The optimism, the cultivated hope, and the promising horizons in the poem's first line, are converted and metamorphosized in the poem's second, following line into bleak, murky, macabre death.

The poem's continuation, however, does not quit surprising. Accordingly, the windows and graves in the speaker's life, celebrating optimizing and deadly darkness change roles, play musical chains. On the one hand, a window is shut for good; indeed, that is exactly the "message" heralded by the run-on-line that opened the poem. There is nothing new about it. But there is something new about the way the morbid, deadly termination turns into promising optimism:

> *"And through the tombstone*
> *I can see*
> *For distance"*

On the one hand, such a statement seems to be devoid of sense; how can one see through a stone, imperforate, obtuse tombstone? On the other hand, however, a tombstone is eternal, is everlasting, is beyond time, and therefore, it redeems the speaker's vision from its mortal limitation while bestowing upon it unearthly capacity. This way, the poem takes advantage of the dynamic nature of the textual continuum (and especially of its effective performance by a "run-on-line") while cultivating a reciprocal, surprising dialogue between two extremes, life and death. And the unexpected interaction between the two extremes confers upon the poem its tense, dense vigor.

*End of the Archaeological Excavation Season in Ein Gedi**

The diggers went home,
They collected their black and white sticks
Everything is measured
They left behind them threads
Like a cobweb.

The Roman archaeological excavation site
Was left wide open on its back
And deserted like a woman who was raped
In the field;

Everything is open and well known
Although she didn't scream.

*An ancient Jewish site close to the Dead Sea.
Today a kibbutz

This poem provides one more worthy display of a prudent, effective usage of the temporal-dynamic nature of the text: a bulk of textual information which is "anchored" in a late (or relatively late) stage of the progressive textual continuum sheds a new light on the way the reader previously comprehended a bulk of textual information which is "anchored" in an earlier stage of the progressive textual continuum.

Correspondingly, the reader is compelled to perform "reverse" reading, to re-read that early bulk of textual information and update (or replace it with a dramatically new one) according to the new light cast by the late bulk of textual information.

The poem in focus consists of two parts, of two stanzas, of two bulks of textual information. The first part, although portraying a situation of termination (the end of the archaeological excavation in Ein Gedi) is certainly of a positive character. Unearthing the distant, misty past that enables us to understand better our history and roots is both rewarding and exciting. The fact that the archaeological excavation season has reached its termination is equally encouraging and gratifying since the lesson which our past has taught us has reached one more advanced stage of elucidation.

The second part of the poem, however, is a simile that metaphorically portrays the poem's first part. That portrayal, however, is drastically surprising as it introduces the first positive part from the most negative, destructive, even repulsive perspective possible. The archaeological dig is metaphorically portrayed as a woman who was thrown on her back and raped in the field. Indeed, she didn't scream. Yet: "everything is open and well known." And nobody extended help to her. Nobody even got close to her.

What could be the reason to shed such a dramatically different light on the evidently positive archaeological excavation? Perhaps to remind us that behind the desirable scientific excitement associated with unearthing the past, that past had been also contaminated and plagued by distasteful, hideous deeds. Our past is like a fabric, like a mosaic. Some parts of it are lofty, uplifting, but other parts of it are abhorrent, abominable. And the clever way this poem enlists the dynamic nature of the textual continuum yields that lesson, the lesson that to our past but should not be forgotten in both our present and our future.

Giving the Torah *

When Moses was sitting
Next to God on the summit of Mount Sinai and writing
On the board.
I was sitting at the very end of the classroom,
in the remote corner
And I was drawing, while feeling like dreaming,
Flowers and faces, airplanes
And ornamented names

Now I show you all:
Don't obey and don't listen!

*Torah: The Pentateuch (Greek: the five scrolls), instruction, teaching, the five books of Moses that according to tradition, Moses received from God on the summit of Mount Sinai

Many similes, metaphors, and images inlaid in Yehuda Amiahai's poetry are remarkably innovative, original, surprising, colorful, even "brave" and daring. Such an image is the following: like a mechanic crawling under a broken car, trying to repair it, God is crawling under the world, trying to repair it. The metaphorical image cultivated and exhibited in this short poem is equally innovative, surprising and "daring." Accordingly, God is depicted as a teacher dictating to his pupil, Moses, the Torah, the Ten Commandments, and the pupil Moses is writing them obediently on the board.

The poem's speaker is also a pupil in that class attended by the pupil Moses. However, while the pupil Moses is thoroughly engaged with the teaching material, with God's delivered lesson, the speaker pupil blatantly detaches himself from the class and from its teacher (God) and His delivered lesson. Accordingly, the speaker pupil is sitting in the most remote corner of the classroom. While being entirely oblivious to Moses the pupil, to God the teacher and His teaching material, the pupil speaker is drawing "flowers and faces, airplanes, and ornamented names.

The pupil speaker concludes the poem with the following warning cry: "Don't obey and don't listen!" That warning cry is neither arbitrary nor random. According to the Torah, when Moses descended Mount Sinai, holding the two stone tablets upon which the Ten Commandments were engraved, he approached the children of Israel and asked them: Will you obey (accept, embrace) the commandments of God? And the children of Israel replied, with no hesitation, with two words only: *na'sseh ve-nishma* (we shall do [accept, obey] and hear [listen]).

The order in which the two words are placed (a compositional-literary device) seems to be surprising, questionable, and wrong. Obeying commandments before even hearing them makes no sense. Hence, first a person hears the commandments and only later does he/she decide whether they are in congruence with him/her, and whether he/she wishes to obey them. However, that illogical order of presentation, that compositional device, yields a rhetorical device (surprise) and that chain of literary devices which are casually connected to each other, conceives a message.

That message reflects the admirable piousness of the children of Israel, their absolute, estimable trust in God: they are willing to obey His commandments even prior to hearing them.

The poem's speaker, however, feels the very opposite. As he preferred to sit in the most remote corner of the classroom, as he preferred to occupy himself with drawing childish drawings instead of listening to the teacher, he prefers not to follow the crowd. He refuses to let the crowd obscure, eclipse, and even erase his own unique being.

Perhaps his own unique being may be humble, perhaps even meek. Yet, this is his own very special, private being and he does not desire that ever be bottled or even clouded. Thus: Don't obey! Don't listen! Follow your heart. Your heart only.

An Eternal Window

Once, being in a garden, I heard
A song on an old blessing.

And above the dark trees
There is a window eternally lit

In memory of the face that once was in it
Which is also a memory of another lit window.

Like in other poems by Yehuda Amichai that include a reference to a window, also in this short poem, the window radiates positive connotations primarily associated with light. The expression "a window eternally lit" (in Hebrew *chalon tamid*) brings to mind both *esh tamid*, eternal fire that was let in the Temple and *ner tamid*, an eternal, memorial candle lit to commemorate the dead.

Hence, that eternal light, and following the eternally lit window, are associated with life. Although that life already extinguished, already faded away, it is still commemorated eternally by the living. Even the commemorated face by the eternally lit window, is also an eternal, memorial light of another lit window. This way the lit windows create a chain of eternal, memorial light that reminds the speaker of the human face that once was enveloped by those lit windows.

And what about the garden? The song? The old blessing? The dark trees? The old blessing can be easily connected to the *ner tamid*, the eternal memorial candle which is lit while reciting a blessing. And that very old blessing the speaker hears is like the window when it is lit, like an eternal, memorial candle.

But what about the garden and the dark trees? Perhaps, perhaps they echo—even very faintly, very feebly—biblical connotations: the garden and the trees where the command of God was breached, where eternal life was taken away, where the let fire of eternal life was extinguished.

And the song? Perhaps the old blessing that is recited in memory of the dead has been converted into the song of the living. After all, the alive speaker is watching the eternally lit window while commemorating the dead. As Nathan Alterman, the highly renowned Hebrew/Israeli poet wrote:

> *"How wonderful, how wonderful are our lives*
> *Which are filled with thoughts of the dead."*
> (From "The Mole")

In an Enchanted Garden

In an enchanted garden, a clean-eyed man is sitting,
Half of him is lit, half of him is forgotten.

His mother called him from a window of slumber,
But he neither slept nor responded
And he went out alone heading away from the fence,
Half of him was still himself, half of him
was already somebody else,

And he loved a famous love story.
And since then he didn't return to the
enchanted garden.

And he lived well and he lived in pain
And if he didn't die yet he is still in love.

It is a pity that the English translation of the poem fails to reflect the attractive rhyme pattern practiced and displayed in the original Hebrew poem. It brings to mind what David Avidan (a highly acclaimed modern Hebrew/Israeli poet) once said: the very essence of a poem gets lost from the moment it is taking off from the runway of its original language until the moment it is landing in the runway of the language of translation. Hence, it is regretful that in order to deliver the content of the translated poem (or any other literary text), too many aesthetic virtues of that poem must be sacrificed.

The man who is sitting in the "enchanted garden" (that may echo the Garden of Eden) is half lit, half- forgotten. Since being lit is associated with being enlightened and therefore being remembered, this man is treading, is striding, in the twilight zone, in no-man's land between remembrance and forgetfulness.

The second stanza reintroduces the window motif, which appears frequently in the poetry of Yehuda Amichai. However, while in those cases the window motif carries and exhibits positive, welcomed connotations (such as optimistic expectations, cultivated promising hopes, open horizons, openness and freedom), the window motif in this poem is associated with slumber that metaphorically reflects morbidity, lifeless termination, death. Yet, those bleak, murky connotations are swiftly challenged by the following line: "But he neither slept nor responded." Accordingly, he did not respond to his mother's cry from a window of slumber since he did not sleep. The continuation, however, does "resurrect" some negative connotations:

> *"And he went out alone away from the fence*
> *Half of him was still himself, half of him was*
> *already somebody else."*

In Jewish tradition, to go away (to go out) of a fence hold considerable negative connotations. To go out of a fence ("*gader*" in Hebrew) in Jewish tradition means to make a breach in the fence of the world (i.e., to open the way to lawlessness), to commit a crime. That and more.

According to Jewish religion, a person who committed suicide must be buried outside of the fence (*gader*) of the graveyard (although this old Jewish religious tradition has not been practiced for numerous years). That and more.

The phrase "half of him was already somebody else" also carries negative connotations. The Hebrew word for "somebody else" is *acher* (which can be translated into "different".) *Acher* in Jewish tradition may stand also for a person who has rejected Judaism, who has "exiled" himself from the Jewish faith. The man in the poem, however, is only half *acher*, since he is still half himself.

Thus, like in the first stanza of the poem, he is treading in a twilight zone, between two contradictory options of existence. Indeed, one may cogently argue that this is also the case in the poem's second stanza. On the one hand, a window of slumber carries deadly negative connotations. On the other hand, however, that man did not sleep, which is evidently positive. Hence, treading in a twilight zone between two contradictory options of human existence, the negative and the positive ones, seems to be an amalgamating thread through the poem's first three stanzas. As will be presently shown, the poem's last stanza does share the very same amalgamating thread (although like in previous stanzas, in the last stanza that amalgamating thread is interwoven differently):

> *"And he loved a famous love story*
> *And since then he didn't return to the enchanted garden."*

Although the first line is quite opaque (how could he love a famous love story? Which love story was that famous love story? What made that love story a famous one?) one may interpret that stanza as follows: That man's love turned into a famous love story and for that reason, he did not need the spellbinding allure of the enchanted garden anymore. The connotations yielded by this stanza are absolutely positive. Yet, the poem's concluding stanza interlaces again the amalgamating thread in which positive and negative connotations are reciprocally interwoven:

> *"And he lived well and he lived in pain*
> *And if he didn't die yet he is still in love."*

The twilight zone in which that man is stepping is surfacing again: his life was both good and bad and there is no certainty that he is still alive. Hence, is he still in the enchanted garden? Or was he exiled from the enchanted garden as Adam and Eve were exiled from their own enchanted garden, the Garden of Eden? Is he still sentenced to be beyond the fence to be the "other," or was he permitted to return to the bosom of society? Is he still half lit and half forgotten? The poem does not provide definite answers to those questions. Indeed; it shouldn't. Treading in a twilight zone of no certainties, of two conflicting options of human existence, is the very essence of this poem, its very credo.

The Fate of God

The fate of God
Is like the fate of
Trees, stones, sun and moon,
Which had not been worshiped anymore
Since people had started worshiping Him.

But He must stay with us:
At least like trees, at least like stones,
At least like the sun, the moon and the stars.

God shares the fate of all non-celestial objects that people quit worshiping: trees, stones, sun, and moon. People worshiped them until they started worshiping God. Now people quit worshiping God. Now people are devoid of faith. Now the world is devoid of faith. Yet, the speaker expresses an urgent wish, indeed, a pressing demand: God must stay with us, at least like the trees, the stones, the sun, the moon, and the stars. Like all those non-celestial objects, which once were heavenly worshiped objects, God must go through a metamorphosis process: to say His last, final farewell to His previous celestial, sacred being, and become an earthly being like the sun, the moon, the stars, the stones and the trees.

Perhaps people don't need their past, total, unconditional faith in heavenly things anymore. Perhaps. But they do need to be embraced by solid, robust, assuring earthly objects; they bestow comfort and a soothing sense of security. The sun, the moon, the stars, the stones, and the trees have done it since they were divorced from their previous celestial role in the lives of human beings. Now it is time for God to echo them.

Gathering Something

In the middle of advancing
Advancing has turned into a withdrawal. But
The direction of the travel
Has not changed. It happened suddenly.
Just like that.

The seams undo.
I, who used to be a hoarder,
A collector,
All which I have collected keeps dropping on the way
Now one can follow me easily.
I am dispensed.

But something of my ancient rustic ancestors
Is still kept inside me:
Now, in the evening, I want to gather
Something, not cattle, not herds.
To gather something.

How can advancing turn into a withdrawal? Only advancing years. The more years are advancing, the more withdrawal of life is progressing: years are advancing, accumulating and the length of life is withdrawing, is lessening and diminishing. Hence, the direction of the travel of life, of life journey, has not changed: the direction of advancing towards termination, towards the deadly ending, is also the direction of the withdrawal's progression, the progression towards the deadly ending.

The seams undo. The seams are ripped. What held life together is torn open, is rent, during the graduating accumulative process of withdrawal, of advancing towards the deadly ending. The seams of life of the speaker, the speaker who used to hoard and collect, fall apart, turn untied, and whatever he hoarded and collected through the advancing years of his life, is hopelessly scattered.

Being alarmed by that unavoidable dispersion, that undefeatable battle, the speaker desires to "resurrect," to revive the gathering instincts of his ancient rustic ancestors. Indeed, unlike them, he does not wish to gather either herds on flocks. Yet, he does wish to gather "something." What is that "something"? Perhaps that "something" is the years which have been left from his life which is fading away, extinguishing, advancing towards its deadly ending.

Following this vein, the poem is a mourning lament of a person who is about to step on the threshold of his life's ending while trying to delay that ending as desperately as possible. But he knows: the termination is lurking in ambush for him, both patiently and deadly.

By My Mother

My mother always calls me from my playing
Outside.
One time she called me
And I returned only after many years
And not from playing.

And now, as I am sitting by her,
She is like silent stones.
All my words and all my poems
Are like an oily flow of words
Of a carport merchant
Of a sleazy, cunning dealer.

The very beginning of the poem introduces its speaker as a child who uses the present tense:

"My mother always calls me from my playing
Outside."

However, in the following line, the present tense turns into past tense and the child speaker turns into an adult speaker:

> *"One time she called me*
> *And I returned only after many years*
> *And not from playing".*

The latter erects a wall of alienation between the speaker and his scolding (although mutely) mother and it equally ignites the adult speaker's ardent desire to appease, to mollify his disapproving mother. His guilty conscience for deserting his mother for many years agonizes him considerably. Hence, he tries to soothe her disapproval, to earn her both understanding and sympathy, by embracing her with his words and poems. Yet, he fails to break through her imperforate wall of cold, undefeatable muteness: "She is like silent stones".

Indeed, the speaker himself does know that his words are devoid of worthy value, they are nothing but a frivolous flow of words, words such those used by a cunning, sleazy dealer. Yet, he only has words in his possession: he has missed his capacity to execute deeds many years ago. Hence, what is left? His haunting, tormenting feelings of guilt, of missing, of loss, his mother's obstinate silence and an unbreachable, thorny barricade that separates them.

The Soldiers in Their Graves

The soldiers in their graves tell us: you, up there,
You who rest wreathes on us,
Like lifebelts made of flowers,
Look at our equal faces
Glancing between our stretched arms. But
Remember the difference that was between us
And the happiness floating upon the water.

Roles are reversed in this poem. Usually those who visit the graves of the soldiers who got killed in battle, "talk" to those dead soldiers by reciting prayers, by uttering words of love and of moving yearning or by wordless, restrained silence. In this poem, however, the dead soldiers are those who speak to their loved ones who came to visit them, to pay respect to them. Their words display a touch of sad irony, however.

The dead soldiers depict the wreathes that are placed on their graves as "lifebelts made of flowers" while no lifebelts in the world can save the dead soldiers. The following statement (also mutely uttered by the dead soldiers) is also saturated with sad irony. They say to their loved ones who came to visit their graves: "Look at our equal faces." Their faces are equal because death robbed them of their uniqueness, of their individuality. Death made them equal.

The arms of the dead soldiers are stretched as if they are pleading with their loving visitors to save them, to redeem them. But their plea is deadly doomed. The dead soldiers continue entreating upon approaching their living, loving visitors: remember the difference that was once between us; remember how once we were like you, living, holding our own individuality, our own uniqueness; remember our gleeful time when we didn't need lifebelts (not even made of flowers) and our bliss was happily floating upon the joyful water of our lives.

Hence, this is a poem of a plea, a poem of supplication, mutely uttered by those who gave their lives for the living, by those who are imploring for even a sliver of remembrance, for a tiny splinter of memory. This is a poem about the humbly expressed plea by the dead who died for a noble cause and who do not desire to be doomed to forgetfulness.

Tourists

They pay us visits of lament and suffocation.
Sitting in the Holocaust museum, showing serious
faces by the Wailing Wall
And laugh behind heavy curtains in fancy hotel rooms

Take pictures with important dead in Rachel tomb site
And in Hertzel tomb site and in*
*Give'at hatachmoshet**
Weep while hearing about the beauty and heroism of
our young ment
Lust after the roughness of our young women
And hang their underwear

For a speedy dry
In a blue, cool, bathtub.

Once I sat on stairs next to the gate of
David's fortress in
Jerusalem and I placed the two heavy
grocery baskets next to me
A group of tourists was standing there
next to the tour-guide
And they used me as a point of reference. "Do you see
that man
With the grocery baskets? A little bit next to the night
of his head
You can see a Roman arch. But he is moving,
he is moving! I said to
Myself; redemption will come only when they will be
told: "Do you see
There the Roman arch? It is not that important;
but next to it, a bit
To the left and below, there is a sitting man who
bought fruits and
Vegetables to his family".

**Theodor Hentzel – The first Zionist Leader*
**Give'at hatachmoshet – a site next to Jerusalem where a bitter, bloody battle was fought in the Six Day War (1967).*

All About Restraint Frustration, About Suppressed Wrath

In not too many poems by Yehuda Amichai, the speaker, whose temper is mild and mellow, displays feelings of frustration (even a restrained one) and wrath. Being mild and mellow by nature, such feelings experienced by Yehuda Amichai's poetic speaker are usually camouflaged prudently, being tamed and bridled carefully.

In this poem, however, the speaker's feelings of frustration and wrath are unmasked, obtrusively unveiled. The frustration and the wrath mutely expressed by the poem's speaker. He is angry at the tourists who pay visits to Jerusalem, who display no interest whatsoever in the people of Jerusalem, the people who live in Jerusalem, who experience Jerusalem on a daily basis, who experience Jerusalem in challenging, testing days of hardship, deprivation, lack, and even agony. The tourists are indifferently oblivious to the "regular" inhabitants of Jerusalem, they pay no attention to them and instead visit "important dead": the gravesite of Rachel (which in reality is the gravesite of an Arab sheikh), the gravesite of Hertzel (the first leader of Zionism), the Holocaust Memorial museum, the site of the fierce battle during the Six-Day War, the Wailing Wall.

And then they erect an impenetrable wall between them and the "real" people of Jerusalem, besiege themselves in the rooms of the luxurious hotels, draw dark heavy curtains and laugh. Laughter, in Biblical Hebrew means many times sexual intercourse (Ishmael, for instance, *metzachek* [laughs] which means, exhibits his sexual maturity that threatens Isaac's birthright and for that reason Sarah evicts him from their tribe; and there are numerous other examples).

The poem's speaker feels humiliated, expelled, used: After the tourists enjoyed "his" Jerusalem without conferring upon him even an ephemeral, hasty look, they exclude him, they leave him out, forcing upon him the humiliating role of the "voyeur" while they are making love.

That is not the end of their sexual lust that stirs the speaker's feelings of humiliation, frustration, and even wrath. The tourists not only weep upon hearing about the beauty and heroism of "our [Israeli] young men" but their also "lust after the roughness of our [Israeli] young women." Indeed, the humiliation, frustration, and the poem's speaker who feels rejected, even defeated, by the tourists who "invaded" his Jerusalem, reach a sexual vertex when the tourists after laughing (making love) in their fancy hotel rooms, being heavy curtains (while leaving out the poem's speaker), "hang their underwear/For a speedy dry/ In a blue, cool bathtub." The underwear that needs washing ignites again the recent memory of love-making from which the frustrated speaker was "evicted" and the cool bathtub reminds him of the scorching heat of Jerusalem to which the speaker is "sentenced." Hence, he feels humiliated, frustrated, defeated for a dense cluster of reasons.

The second stanza of the poem is composed as prose while rendering an ideological/moral/historical lesson. The tired speaker, laden with two heavy baskets filled with fruits and vegetables that he just bought in the market, was sitting for a rest on the stairs, next to the gate of David's Tower in Jerusalem, A group of tourists clustered next to a town guide who used the speaker as a point of reference. He told the tourists: "the Roman Arch is just next to the man with the baskets. "And the speaker said to himself; redemption will come only when they [the tourists] will be told: "Do you see there the Roman Arch? It is not that important; but next to it, a bit to the left and below, there is a sitting man who bought fruits and vegetables to his family."

Indeed, this second, prose stanza complements the previous, first one: the "heroic" monuments should not eclipse the humanistic importance of the individual. The historical memorials, obelisks, pillars, and relics, despite their undebated glory and importance, should never cloud the prominence of the human being. The tourists in the first stanza let the splendor of stones and monuments in Jerusalem cast a shadow on the people of Jerusalem.

In this unfortunate way the voice of humanism is muted, the Gospel of humanism is denied and defiled. And the poetry of Yehuda Amichai heralds humanism at its very best, places humanism on the highest pedestal.

SOME COMMENTS OF CONCLUSION

Yehuda Amicahi died prematurely in 2000. But his poems did not die with him. His poems continue—and will continue—living vitally, vividly for numerous years to come. His poems will always continue living in the hearts of dozens of thousands of people who wholeheartedly adore his poems, whose poems touch their hearts and souls profoundly. His poems will continue living in the hearts and minds of the literary scholars who probe them. And his poems will continue living in the hearts and minds of the literary critics who evaluate his poems.

The poems of Yehuda Amicahi will continue living for countless years due to their novel, surprising aesthetic creativity, due to their humanist sensitivity that touches the variegated, ramified spectrum of human feelings and experiences: love, frustrated love, hope, hopeless experiences, passion, compassion, desire, sexual lust, soothing promises, cultivated expectations, blatantly breached expectations, piercingly bitter disappointment, pain engraved in an unkind memory of consuming, brazen experiences, unveiling the haunting, tormenting past, nourishing gratifying hopes for the future, sweet memories from pacified, unblemished childhood, the brutal horrors of the wars, his unconditional love for his country, for its people, the passionate love for Jerusalem, for the Israeli desert, the elevated level of the most lofty humanism, placing the individual on the highest pedestal, a refusal to surrender to the popular “decrees” dictated by the masses, a refusal to tolerate even a sliver of authoritarian edict.

And humility. Humility that sprouts from inner strength, from inner firm self conviction. Humility that only a strong poet like Amichai can afford and practice. Humility that can be forged only in the poetic workshop of a poet like Yehuda Amichai. Humility that does not bud from weakness. Humility that is the very vertex of sweeping strength. And above all love. “Love is all he needs.” And love is all he seeks.

Yehuda Amichai’s poems could be portrayed as a bottomless quarry of love. All the above will ensure that Yehuda Amichai’s death will not dictate the death of his poems. They will never be forgotten, they will never be forsaken. His enticing aesthetic legacy will never fade away. Will never be afflicted by forgetfulness. The world of poetry could not find a better harbinger to herald the very essence of poetry in its very vertex. A gifted, praiseworthy harbinger like Yehuda Amichai.

And let us say Amen.

List of Poems

G

H

I

L

M

N

O

P

R

S

T

W

BIBLIOGRAPHY

Alter, Robert. *The Poetry of Yehuda Amichai.* Ferrar, Straus and Giroux, N.Y. 2015

Abramson, Glenda. *The Writing of Yehuda Amichai: A Thematic Approach.* State University of New York Press. N.Y., 1989

Avneni Shraga. "The Poems of Yehuda Amichai" (in Hebrew) Mevo't, 1, January 1955

Alter, Robert. "Poetry in Israel" Commentary, December 1965.

Arad, Airiam. "Amichai's Poetry Begins to Mellow". *Jerusalem Post Weekly,* 12, May 1969.

Arad, Miriam. "Yehuda Amichai Looks Back". *Jerusalem Post,* 10, May 1963

Alter, Robert. *After the Tradition.* New York; E.P. Dutton, 1969.

Banzel, Hillel. "The Sweet tLaments of Yehuda Amichai" (in Hebrew). *Yedi'ot Achnonot,* 25, October 1974.

Be'er Hayim. "The Poetry Volume "Now at Noise" by Yehuda Amichai" (in Hebrew). *Ha'anetz,* 21, March 1969.

Beardsley, C.M. *Aesthetics.* Brace World, N.Y. 1958

Banzel, Hillel. "The Existential Trend in Our Poetry" (in Hebrew). *Ha'aretz,* November 25, 1960.

Cohen, Bo'az. "Don't Call me a National Poet" (in Hebrew). Interview with Yehuda Amichai. *Yedi'ot Achronot,* September 24, 2000.

Don, Moshe. "Not to Praise" (in Hebrew). *Ma'riv,* 1, October 1971.

Empson, William. *Some Versions of Pastoral.* N. D Paperbook, London, 1950.

Empson, Williams. *Seven Types of Ambiguity.* Chatto and Windus, London, 1963

Eliot, T.S. *The Sacred Wood: Essays on Poetry and Criticism.* Methuer, London, 1920.

Feingold, Ben-Ami. "Amichai 1948-1962" (in Hebrew). *Haboker,* 24, May 1963.

Fentom, James. "Time by Yehuda Amichai" *London Review of Books 6*, December 1979.

Frye, Northrop. *Anatomy of Criticism*. Princeton University Press. 1957.

Gazit, ze'v. "About the Poems by Yehuda Amichai" (in Hebrew). *Unim*, May 1967.

Gold, Scharf, Nili. "And the Vows are not Vows: On Amichais Later Poetry" (in Hebrew). *Siman Kni'a*, 22 (1991), 361-378.

Gold Scharf, Nili. *Not Like a Cypress: Transformations of Images and Structures in the Poetry of Yehuda Amichai* (in Hebrew). Schocker, Tel Aviv, 1994.

Gold Scharf, Nili. "Images in Transformation in Recent Poetry by Yehuda Amichai". *Prooftexts 4* (1984). 141-152.

Gold Scharf Nili. Yehuda Amichai. *The Making of Israel's National Poet*. Brandeis University Press, Waltham, Massachusetts, 2008.

Hirsch, E.D. *Validity of Interpretation*. Yale University Press, New Haven, 1952.

Iser, Wolfgang. *The Implied Reader*. Johns Hopkins University Press, Baltimore and London, 1974.

Kreitler, Hans, Kreitler, Shulamit. *The Psychology of the Arts*. Durham, N.C. 1976.

Lessing, G.E. *Laocoon*. The Monday Press, New York, 1957.

Mazor, Yair. *Israeli Poetry of the Holocaust*. Fairleigh Dickinson University Press, New York, 2009.

Mazor, Yair. *Poetic Acrobat: The Poetry of Ronny Someck*. Goblin Fern Press, Madison, 2008.

Mazor, Yair. *Broken Twig: The Hebrew Poetry of Dalia Rabikowitz*. Maven Mark Books, Milwaukee, 2013.

Midlin, Mein. "Major Poetic Even". *Jerusalem Post*, 9, May 1958

Mazor, Yair. *A Sense of Structure: Hebrew and Biblical Literature* (in Hebrew). University Publishing Projects. Tel Aviv, 1987.

Mazor, Yair. *From Wooded Meadows to Downtown Tel Aviv. Contemporary Hebrew Poetry* (in Hebrew). Papyrus Press of Tel Aviv University, Tel Aviv, 1996

Mazor, Yair. *From Medieval Spain to the Land of Cinderella: Studies in Hebrew Poetry and in Hebrew Children's Poetry* (in Hebrew). Tag, Tel Aviv, 1996.

Mazor, Yair. *Pain, Pining and Pine Trees: Contemporary Hebrew Poetry.* Papyrus Press of Tel Aviv University, Tel Aviv, 2000.

Mazor, Yair. *Love in the Back Seat: Hebrew Poetry in the 1960s* (in Hebrew). Zmora – Bitan, Tel Aviv, 2005.

Mazor, Yair. *Bridled Bird: The Hebrew Poetry of Nathan Zach.* Maven Mark Books, Milwaukee, 2013.

Mazor, Yair. *Nocturnal Lament: The Poetry of David Fogel the Harbinger of Modern Hebrew Poetry.* Maven Mark Books, Milwaukee, 2013.

Mazor, Yair. *The Flower and the Fury: The Hebrew Poetry of Yona Wollach.* Maven Mark Books, Milwaukee, 2013.xxx

Mazor, Yair. *A Poet Writes the Blues: The Hebrew Poetry of Ronny Someck.* Maven Mark Books, Milwaukee, 2016.

Mazor, Yair. *Under a Silky Sky: The Hebrew Symbolist Poetry of Edith Convensky.* Maven Mark Books, Milwaukee, 2015

Mazor, Yair. "Besieged Feminism in Contemporary Hebrew Poetry: Contradictory Rhetorical Trends in the Poetry of Dalia Rabikowitz". *World Literature Today* (1985), Vol. 58, No. 4, pp. 354-359.

Mazor, Yair. "Farewell to Arms and Sentimentality: Reflections of Israel's Wars in Yehuda Amichai's Poetry". *World Literature Today,* (1986), Vol.60, No.1, pp.12-17.

Mazor, Yair. "Contemporary Israeli Poetry: Yehuda Amichai's 'Connect' Poem, on: Portrait of a Poet as a Master of Sentiment". *Cincinnati Judaica Review* (1991) Vol.3, pp. 62-69.

Mazor, Yair. "Portrait of Sadness as a One-Way Ticket: Yehuda Amichai's Poetry". (in Hebrew). HaDo'ar (1994), Vol.73, No.1, pp. 19 -21.

Mazor, Yair. "Like a Natural Path in the Desert: 'Aesthetic Engineering' in Yehuda Amichai's Poetry" (in Hebrew) (1994) HaDo'ar, Vol.73, Nos. 8-9, pp. 20-22;21-23.

Mazor, Yair. "Swindling Simplicity in Yehuda Amicahi's Poetry" (in Hebrew)(1994), Moznayim Vol.69, No.5, pp. 8-11

Mazor, Yair. "Only now, when the Dust Has Settled: Hebrew Poetry in the 1960th" (in Hebrew)(1996). Iton 77, Vol. 198, No. 19, pp. 20-23.

Mazor, Yair. "Class Reunion: More Aspects of Hebrew Poetry in the 1960th" (In Hebrew) (2001) Iton 77, Vol.25, No. 253, pp. 15-20.

Nimrod, Noah. "A Hebrew Poet Abroad". *Jewish Chronicle* (London), 29, August 1959.

Nagid, Hayim. "I Think that this Land is Paradise For Poets". Interview with Yehuda Amichai. Ma'aniv, April 14, 1977.

Rabinowitz, Osnat. "A Woman Through a Poet's Perspective". Dvar Hapoe'lt, May-June, 1976, 60-61.

Riffaterre, Michael. *Semiotics of Poetry*. Indiana University Press, Bloomington, 1978.

Smith Herrnstein, Barbara. *Poetic Closure: A Study of How Poems End*. Chicago University Press, Chicago 1968.

Striedter, Junij. "The Russian Formalist Theory of Literary Evolution". P.T.L. 3, No.1 (1978), 1-24.

Sadan-Lubenstein, Niki. "Imagistic Patterns in the Poetry of Yehuda Amichai (in Hebrew). Iton 77 (1983), 89-99.

Wellek, René. *Concepts of Criticism*. Yale University Press, New Haven, 1967.

Yudkin, Leon. *Escape into Siege*. London: Routledge & Kagan Paul, 1974.

Young Vernon. "It Makes You Wonder: Time: Poems by Yehuda Amichai". *New York Review of Books*, 22, November 1970.

Zach, Nathan. "The Light Muse" (in Hebrew), Davar, August 28, 1959.

ABOUT THE AUTHOR

Dr. Yair Mazor is Professor Emeritus of modern Hebrew and Biblical literature at the University of Wisconsin–Milwaukee. To date, Professor Mazor has authored 28 scholarly books and more than 250 articles and critical essays that have been published in the USA, Israel, and numerous European countries. Dr. Mazor is a popular guest lecturer and has spoken to audiences throughout Europe and many other venues around the world.

Among the many scholarly awards Dr. Mazor has received are the Sadan Prize and the Shpan Prize for two of his books, the Baron Prize for Excellency in the field of Jewish studies, the distinguished teaching award by the University of Wisconsin–Milwaukee, and the Friedman Prize, a national award for the most distinguished Hebrew literature scholar in the United States.

In his military service, Dr. Mazor acted as a combat paratrooper, as well as an instructor of parachuting.

www.ingramcontent.com/pod-product-compliance
Lightning Source LLC
Chambersburg PA
CBHW070348090426
42733CB00009B/1336